THE SCANDINAVIAN GUIDE TO HAPPINESS

THE SCANDINAVIAN GUIDE TO HAPPINESS

THE NORDIC ART OF HAPPY AND BALANCED LIVING WITH FIKA, LAGOM, HYGGE, AND MORE

BY TIM RAYBORN

The Scandinavian Guide to Happiness

13-digit ISBN: 978-1-95151-121-0
10-digit ISBN: 1-95151-121-2

This book may be ordered by mail from the publisher. Please include $5.99 for postage and handling. Please support your local bookseller first!

Books published by Whalen Book Works are available at special discounts when purchased in bulk. For more information, please email us at info@whalenbookworks.com.

Whalen Book Works
68 North Street
Kennebunkport, ME 04046
www.whalenbookworks.com

Cover and interior design by Bryce de Flamand
Typography: Gill Sans MT Pro, Sackers Gothic Std, and Sabon LT Pro
All images licensed from Shutterstock

Printed in China
2 3 4 5 6 7 8 9 0

"Contentment is the only real wealth."

—ALFRED NOBEL

CONTENTS

INTRODUCTION

Are you curious why Sweden, Denmark, Norway, Finland, and Iceland consistently rank among the top ten happiest countries on earth? In this book, you'll learn some of the secrets to their happiness and fulfillment. You'll explore centuries of Nordic wisdom, from the modern age back to the time of the Vikings—who were often less fierce than some histories have made them out to be!

What is it about these countries that makes many of their people seem so content and happy, despite living in regions that are frequently cold and dark for a good portion of the year? As you'll see, there are several answers to this question, encompassing many areas of culture, society, and life. Each chapter explores one aspect of Nordic well-being, focusing on a different country, and gives suggestions for how you can easily bring these ideas and practices into your own life, no matter where you live.

- **LAGOM** is a Swedish concept meaning just the right amount—not too much, not too little.
- **FRILUFTSLIV** is the Norwegian word for the joy of experiencing nature.

- **FIKA** is the Swedish daily coffee break that lets you slow down a little.
- **HYGGE** is the Danish love of coziness, which brings comfort, security, and happiness.
- **LYKKE** is the Danish belief that happiness is all around you, if you know where to look.
- **SISU** is the Finnish dedication to cultivating everyday courage, grit, determination, and being prepared in the face of adversity.
- **ÞETA REDDAST** is the enduring Icelandic belief that everything will work out.

Adopting these basic principles may help you have a happier and more satisfying life without spending a lot of money, making big changes in your life (unless you want to!), or doing anything else too drastic. If anything, taking these ideas on board will help you look for places to simplify and un-complicate your life, advice that we all need more of these days. You'll learn about the Nordic perspective on topics such as simplicity, contentment, health and wellness, perseverance, work-life balance, nature-inspired living, and more.

And in case you were wondering, the term *Scandinavian* generally refers to Denmark, Sweden, and Norway, while *Nordic* is usually a broader term that includes those nations, along with Finland, Iceland, and the Faroe Islands. As more and more people are discovering, these countries and cultures have much to teach us about living happier, healthier, more fulfilling lives.

The Covid-19 pandemic has left many feeling stressed, anxious, and uncertain. Therefore, some of the time-honored suggestions about getting together with friends and family may be difficult or impossible when one is practicing social distancing. But that shouldn't make you put off trying those things that you can do safely and innovating on other practices. Can a cozy evening of hygge be had via video chat? There's no reason why not! And many practices, such as experiencing friluftsliv outdoors by oneself, seem tailor-made for these troubling times.

So, if you'd like to bring some of these wise and timeless ideas into your own life, let this guide get you started!

CHAPTER 1

Lagom

Just the Right Amount—
Not Too Much, Not Too Little

(PRONOUNCED "LAH-GOM")

SWEDEN

“A wise person does all things in moderation.”

—GISLI SURSSON’S SAGA

Lagom means "just the right amount," and refers to the wisdom of moderation. There is a Swedish proverb that says, *Lagom är bäst*, which literally means, "the right amount is best." The idea is to keep things in balance and not give in to excesses in any area of life. This concept is very old in Nordic societies. According to the sayings of Odin from the thirteenth-century Hávamál: "Hold the cup but drink the mead moderately. Speak sensibly or be silent." We can probably think about those times when we indulged too much in alcohol and suffered a headache the next day because of it, said things we shouldn't have, or ate an entire bar of chocolate and felt pretty sick afterward! Sticking to the philosophy of lagom would help us to avoid these missteps (and the side effects!).

But lagom extends to society as well and can mean a desire for equity and fairness. Reckless consumerism and hoarding can cause great amounts of pain and suffering, and should be avoided. When there is not enough to go around, there is imbalance. But lagom is not a call to communism; it's simply a way of looking at things reasonably and trying to keep perspective on what's fair and what works best in society. On a personal level, it's about keeping one's head straight and coming to a consensus to live in harmony with others. As such, it's a very important concept in Swedish society and life.

It's also about slowing things down and enjoying the life that you have around you, in the moment. It means taking time out for yourself and your loved ones, and not going to extremes; working twelve hours a day is helping no one, will badly affect your health, and will cause you to lose precious time with your friends and family that you'll never get back. Rein it in, work a normal workday, and take the time to appreciate the little things that make all of our lives so worth living. If your job is demanding that kind of extra commitment, then it's time to seriously think about moving on to something else. It's never worth sacrificing your health and all your time for work, even if you think you have a lofty goal in the distance. That goal will never materialize in the exact way you want it, and once you get addicted to that kind of overachievement and the short-term dopamine hits you can get from it, you'll probably never be free of it. Practicing lagom demands having a better work-life balance right now, and once you start it, you'll be glad you did. No one on their deathbed ever thinks, "I wish I'd worked more," but they do regret the time they lost, not appreciating the days before they all sailed by. And many people regret not saying the things they wish they'd said to loved ones.

But living a life more in harmony with this idea isn't something you have to extensively plan out and put lots of work into; that would defeat the whole purpose! Lagom can be as simple as taking a nice lunch break, reading a good book, enjoying fika with friends (see chapter 3), or getting out and enjoying time in nature (see chapter 2). On a personal level, you may feel out of balance in your own life in lots of simple ways: Do you have too many old clothes cluttering up your closet? It would most definitely be lagom to clear some of them out and free up the space. Are you holding on to old papers that you no longer need? Try to get rid of them. Are you not eating as well as you'd like? Take some small steps (that you'll stick with) to correct that. Do you spend too much money going out to restaurants and bars? Try doing that a little less each week.

As you can see, lagom is not a drastic, life-changing way of behaving (it's OK to indulge in a piece of chocolate cake once in a while). Lagom is about making little changes here and there that can make your life feel more balanced. Here are some ideas that you can put into practice right now to help get you started!

THE LAGOM WORK-LIFE BALANCE

Swedes are known for working hard, but not so hard that they sacrifice everything else for it. When the day ends, they leave. That's it. If someone insists on working at the office late, it's usually met with some concern, and the manager might even intervene and ask if everything is OK. That's a refreshing take for Americans, who have been known to clock up to sixty (!) hours a week or more on work projects. If that kind of schedule bothers you, it should, and you're not alone.

Work is important, but it can't be the only thing you have. This is not lagom. If you're putting in that many extra hours and feeling tired, run-down, and sick, it's time to step back and establish some new boundaries. Obviously, going the extra mile occasionally can be good for your company and your own reputation, but your own health matters, too. To be clear: your job is *not* worth sacrificing your family, friends, and health over. It just isn't. Knowing when to say no to things is crucial to keeping that balance. Here are some ideas.

- **LEAVE WORK WHEN THE DAY IS DONE.** That doesn't mean you need to dash out the door at three seconds past the closing hour, but be ready to finish up and leave. Unless there's a fiendish deadline looming, it's OK to put some things off until tomorrow. It really is. Your time off is yours, and you need it to relax and recuperate. Don't feel guilty about this. You have value beyond your occupation.

- <u>BE OK WITH LETTING THINGS GO.</u> Sometimes "good enough" really is. Getting caught up in tiny details will only slow you down and delay your projects. Of course, some things have to be done with precision. But if you find yourself stressing over small details so much that the project isn't finished on time, then you'll probably need to loosen up a bit. Worse, you might be taking things home to work on. There are only so many hours in the day, and you deserve some of them to yourself.

- <u>TAKE TIME AT HOME TO REALLY UNPLUG FROM THE DAY.</u> You may have been staring at a computer screen all day, so don't just come home and do the same thing all night. As you'll see in the fika and hygge chapters, there's great value in disconnecting and having time that's solely for you. Music, food you like, a glass of wine . . . be creative and learn to let the world be for a while.

- CONSIDER MORE PHYSICAL ACTIVITY. If your job is mainly sedentary (i.e., sitting at a desk all day), it's a great idea to get out for a short walk or do something else that gets you moving. You don't have to go invest in a gym membership, unless you want to. Be realistic about what you think you can do and will continue doing. Countless studies show that any activity at all will improve our moods and overall state. You can do a lot of it during your workday: get off the bus a stop early and walk, take the stairs instead of the elevator, ask for a standing desk, take a walk at lunch. Check out the friluftsliv chapter for some ideas for what to do if you want to go out on walks around your neighborhood, or to a local park.

- MAKE TIME FOR SLEEP. Really, make time for it. If you have to be up early to get into your workplace, make sure you go to bed early enough the night before to allow for a good amount of sleep. Power down the computer and the phone at least an hour before going to bed, and do something else: read, meditate, take a bath, snuggle . . . whatever works for you. Healthy adults need at least six to seven hours of sleep a night. If you're getting less than that, you're going to start having health problems at some point. In the US, up to 70 million adults report sleep issues, and even in

Sweden the number of people having trouble getting enough sleep has doubled in the last twenty years. Clearly, none of us are immune from this problem, so we each have to take steps to correct it. Otherwise, "sleeping when you're dead" may become all too true!

- **SET ASIDE TIME FOR SOMETHING THAT'S UNIQUELY YOURS.** Whatever it may be—painting, reading, gardening, playing the guitar—take the time to indulge in it a little bit every day, if you can. It can be a part of part of your hygge experience, which will only enhance the mood. It's important not to let your responsibilities get in the way of doing the things that really bring you joy. Take out a piece of paper and write down what you like doing, or what you might like to try. Then commit to doing a little more of them each week. These don't need to be grand plans and excursions. Telling yourself that you'd like to learn how to knit or improve your cooking skills are examples of keeping things manageable. Remember, it's for fun, not a competition against yourself.

- **TAKE A DAY OR HALF-DAY OFF ONCE IN A WHILE.** Depending on what you do for a living, this may or may not be feasible. But if it's possible to get away, or even work from home sometimes, do it. A change of scene and a bit more variety will probably help you do better at your job, anyway. Sweden has been experimenting for some time with more flexible work schedules and shorter (six-hour) working days. It's estimated that only 1 percent or less of people work fifty hours a week or more. Sweden also has generous vacation time (up to twenty-five days a year), and long maternity and paternity leave options (480 days of paid leave split between two parents).

- **DISCONNECT PROPERLY WHEN YOU'RE ON VACATION.** Don't be available to discuss crises as they come up; arrange for someone else to handle it while you're gone. Don't be tempted by texts and emails from someone who needs "just a few minutes of your time." Don't think about ways you could improve *xyz* when you get back. Unplug. Be in the moment. Free time for yourself is far too rare for you to give up even more of it out of some misguided sense of duty. Work will be there when you return, but if you burn out and ruin your health, you may not get it back. And if your job can't function properly function without you there, it's time to make some major changes. Be good to yourself.

Spend a few weeks putting some of these ideas into action, and make a commitment to see them through. You may begin to notice that you feel more balanced and less stressed when you disconnect from the busy world and the chaos that are always going on around you.

DEVELOPING LAGOM WITH FAMILY AND FRIENDS

It's crucial to remember those in your life who are most important to you. One of the most important ways that we maintain a healthy feeling of balance in our lives is to reach out to family and friends, both in good times and bad. If you aren't available, bring work home every night, or are too tired to see the ones who matter most, you have a problem. Time lost can never be regained, so try to modify that as soon as you can.

Numerous studies have shown that having good family and friend ties can be essential for our health. One European study showed stronger social ties could lead to a 50 percent higher survival rate! So, it seems entirely in the spirit of lagom and moderation that spending more quality time with loved ones will be good for all of you. If you want to set aside more time and bring this part of your life into more balance, here are some ideas to get you started.

- GO AHEAD AND ASK. Don't wait for others to do the planning and arranging. Take the initiative and reach out. This can be to close friends, family members, or even people you haven't talked to in a while. Check in with them, see how they're doing, and get the communication going.
- DON'T OVERTHINK GETTING TOGETHER. Meeting up with loved ones doesn't have to involve a lot of expense and extensive planning. As you'll see in chapter 4, hygge emphasizes simplicity above all. What's important is the experience itself. Skip the fancy dinner and meet up in a park. Invite people over and have each person bring their own snacks. Keep it simple and fun. The less of a hassle it is, the more likely people will want to be a part of it. Make sure that if you commit to something, you actually go through with it!
- USE TIME TOGETHER TO WORK ON OTHER THINGS. Not every get-together can always be a fun party. Why not do things like go grocery

shopping for the week together, or have a group laundry session? Maybe help each other out by cleaning each other's homes, rotating to a new place every Sunday. You can have a nice socializing/chore balance that gets things done but also lets you interact and have fun. If you can't get together in person, try meeting up on a phone or video call while you're working on something else. Chat on the phone while you dust. Have a video call while you clear out old stacks of paper. Make your boring chores something to look forward to!

- SET ASIDE SOME "MICRO-TIMES" FOR PEOPLE. You can't always be available when you'd like, but taking 30 seconds to send an email or text letting someone know that you're thinking of them can be a lovely way to brighten up their day and strengthen your connection.

- SHOW OTHERS WHAT THEY MEAN TO YOU. Special events like birthdays and anniversaries are only here once, and then they're gone. A key part of reclaiming balance in your life is to make sure that you can be present for important occasions as often as possible. You want to be able to feel that you're there for others, and the happiness that brings you and them will stay with you.

If work is always pulling you away, it's time to consider making changes. The regrets you'll have later aren't worth the time you're losing and the money you're getting now.

LAGOM AND YOUR HEALTH

In addition to the benefits you can gain from keeping a better work-life balance and having quality time with friends and family, it's important to take care of yourself. Your health and mental well-being are crucial to everything; nothing else much will matter if either of these is under stress and strain. In addition to increasing your exercise and getting more sleep, here are some suggestions for bringing more balance into that most personal of places, your own body and mind.

- **WATCH WHAT YOU EAT.** You knew this was coming, didn't you? But this doesn't mean you have to adopt a Spartan diet or give up the things you love; just be more mindful of the effects that some foods have on you. Do you have any food allergies? Do some foods leave you feeling bloated or off? Become aware of these and try to reduce or eliminate them from your diet. Eat more vegetables, but get creative about how you prepare them. Try going meat-free a day or two a week. Cut down on sugar and bad fats. Basically, all the things you're used to hearing. Remember that it's OK to indulge sometimes in the foods you love—just take a bit more care about how often you do.

- **WATCH WHAT YOU DRINK.** If you do drink alcohol, that's fine; indulging in a bit can be a great part of hygge, as you'll see. But be careful as you get older to moderate your intake. What you used to be able to do in college, you won't be able to do in your forties; it's just a fact of life. When it comes to alcohol, focus on quality, rather than quantity. Don't chug four beers; find a really good, delectable brew that you can savor over the course of the evening. Share a better bottle of wine with friends and watch how it changes over the course of an evening. Make alcohol more special.

- **WATCH WHAT YOU DRINK, PART TWO.** Gulping down huge sugar-filled sodas or coffees several times a day is fine when you're in your teens or twenties but will probably have longer-term health effects as you get older. And if you're in your twenties right now, use this as a message to start moderating it today. We like to joke about caffeine addiction, but it's actually a problem that can cause issues later on. Remember, lagom is not about giving things up; it's about moderation. As with alcohol, think quality over quantity. Drink less coffee but make each one count. Don't just consider it fuel; take the time to actually savor the aroma, the flavor, the total experience. When you delve into the delights of fika (see chapter 3), you'll see how savoring that coffee can be a truly indulgent experience.

- EAT A LITTLE LESS. We've been conditioned to clean our plates, but this can soon lead to overindulgence. We take more food than we need at the buffet and turn every day into a veritable Thanksgiving feast. But our systems do better if they're not overloaded with so much food at one time. Some people advocate for eating six smaller meals a day, but if this is not feasible for you, stick with your three, but be more aware of how much you're eating. Stop eating when you're full; it sounds simple, but all too often, we don't do it. Consider trying an intermittent fast. This is a simple thing you can do once a week or more, as you see fit. Basically, pick one day and confine all of your eating to an eight-hour period (say, 9:00 a.m. to 5:00 p.m.). Yes, you'll feel hungry, and that's the point. Feeling true hunger puts you back in touch with your body and your needs. Research is starting to show that regular intermittent fasting may be good for health and weight maintenance. Always check with your doctor before you try any new diets or exercise, or if you have any concerns.

- TRY MEDITATING. You don't need to become a yogi to enjoy the benefits of meditation. This book contains various simple meditations that can be used to bring about a sense of calm and well-being wherever you are, at any time of the day. Countless studies have proven the benefits of meditation on the mind and the body. It's something simple you can do for yourself at any time that doesn't require any props or financial outlay and can bring you real benefits.

- BE KIND TO YOURSELF. If you are under stress or feeling depressed or unhappy, be sure to attend to these problems. There is no shame at all in seeking out counseling or therapy if you need it. You might choose to contact a professional, or simply spend time with a friend or family member and talk about what's on your mind. Don't neglect your mental health or simply try to push through when times get tough. Lagom is about being kind to yourself in body and mind.

- **REACH OUT TO HELP OTHERS.** One of the best ways to bring ourselves happiness and a feeling of balance is to do good for others. The Swedish have a reputation for being welcoming to refugees, for example. If you have the time and are capable of volunteering, consider giving a few hours a week to a cause you believe in. You help them out and the effort makes you feel good, so everyone wins! There are loads of ways to help that don't have to involve going someplace in person. Does a charity need help with admin or emailing? Does a community center or library need press releases written? Look around and see if there are organizations in your own community that could use your helping hand.

We're all concerned about health issues, but so often, people can overlook simple things they can do to take some control over them. Of course, always seek the advice of a doctor or other qualified professional if you have concerns, but even making some of these small changes can have a beneficial effect on your overall health.

LAGOM IN THE HOME

As you can imagine, lagom in the home is about bringing a feeling of simplicity and balance into your surroundings. Yes, this means you might be faced with decluttering! But it's something most of us feel like we need to do, so if you're making a commitment to try to remove excess, why not do the same in your living space? Nordic design is often about simplicity, and while some may consider it to be sparse, there is great wisdom in having more free space and not being weighed down with things. If you'd like to give your home a lagom makeover, here are some ideas for how to do it.

- **DECIDE WHAT YOU COULD ACCEPT HAVING LESS OF.** Quite a few of us are hoarders in our own way. If there are things that you know you don't need, make a list. You may have an impressive closet of clothes or shoes, but how often have you worn some of them in the last year? Two years? Longer? If you can't remember, it's time to let them go.

- **DO A LITTLE EVERY DAY.** Don't get overwhelmed. If you haven't even looked in the back of your closet in several years, there's going to be more in there than you can face in one go!

Commit a little time each day to simplifying your surroundings. Take ten to fifteen minutes, at most.

- **FOCUS ON ONE SPACE OR ROOM AT A TIME.** It can feel overwhelming to face clearing a whole house, or even an apartment, so don't let the size of it all get you down. As with limiting your time each day, limit the area that you'll be working on. This isn't a mad dash to get everything out in a week. You acquired loads of stuff (junk) over a long time, so it won't disappear overnight.
- **DECIDE WHERE THE CLUTTER CAN GO.** You may be able to donate a decent number of things to thrift stores. A few more valuable items might be things you can sell (and we all can use some extra cash now and then). Paper can be recycled, and some other things you may have no choice but to throw out. But try to find a second life or at least a decent end for things before just throwing them away. Part of adopting lagom is also being more responsible about our resources.
- **MAKE IT HARDER FOR NEW CLUTTER TO ACCUMULATE.** If you always pile paper up on the coffee table or a nightstand, put something else in those places so that you'll have nowhere

to let a new pile start to grow. If you have dozens of spare hangers for clothes, donate them or give them away to friends. By limiting the chances for new clutter to take hold, you can get in the habit of stopping it before it starts.

- COMMIT TO BUYING LESS. This is good advice overall, for your wallet and your living space! When you do make purchases, try buying nice things that are secondhand. Lagom is very much about not being wasteful, and you can often get amazing deals on furniture and other household items that have been gently used. These pieces can help with the sense of hygge that you'll want to create (see chapter 4), and represent the balance of not indulging in the newest, most expensive thing just for the sake of it.

- MAKE AN EFFORT TO KEEP YOUR HOME CLEAN. Annoyingly, the more often you do this, the easier it will be! A little bit of cleaning, dusting, wiping down the sink, etc., every few days will do a lot to keep your place looking cleaner, and you feeling better about it. Make your bed every day, or at least pull the covers and duvet up and smooth them out. Clean up spills on countertops or the stove as they happen. The point is to keep it from getting to the stage of being an overwhelming chore.

- **LEAVE YOUR SHOES AT THE DOOR.** It's amazing how many germs and bacteria your outside shoes can carry into a home; really, it's pretty gross. In Sweden, it's common—even mandatory—to remove your shoes and leave them at the entry. This is a good practice to bring into your own living space. Get a small shoe rack or other suitable place to store outside shoes, and make sure there's enough room for guests' shoes, too. Have a dedicated pair of house slippers, wear a cozy pair of socks, or go barefoot in hot weather. Shoes can also scuff floors and wear down carpets much faster, so you'll be preserving your décor and saving money.

LAGOM IN THE WORLD

Being mindful of not using too much in the bigger scheme of things is increasingly an issue that we all must face. It's not just enough to bring balance into our own lives and homes; we need to think about our impact collectively on the wider world. The philosophy of "not too little, not too much" can be a solution to many of the bigger problems and crises now facing us. Here are a few more ideas for how you can do your part and make lagom a community idea.

- **COMMIT TO USING FEWER RESOURCES.** Throw out less garbage, use less water (shorter showers and more efficient washing techniques), use less electricity (turn off anything you're not using, including lights and plug strips). Pretty much all the things you've heard about for conservation apply here and are a part of modern lagom. Each person is only one small part of the picture, but together it can have a huge impact.

- **HELP YOUR NEIGHBORHOOD.** In addition to volunteering for your favorite charity, look around in your own neighborhood and see who might need help, or what could use some community effort. Is there a little problem? Do people feel unsafe at night? Is it worth trying to get residents to meet on a regular basis to discuss local concerns? There may already be a group for this. If so, find out what you can do to help out. They would certainly appreciate an extra pair of hands!

- **HELP YOUR WORKPLACE.** Is there anything in your office or workplace that would benefit from decluttering? From being more energy efficient?

Talk with your boss or manager and see if there are simple things you can put into practice that will help simplify the space so that employees feel lighter and less overwhelmed by complexity and clutter. That can only help everyone in the long run, and your company may appreciate your efforts to improve morale and productivity.

- START OR TAKE PART IN A COMMUNITY GARDEN. Small plots are showing up all over the place, where neighbors can grow herbs and vegetables to share with everyone. If you live in a place where you can't have your own garden, this can be an especially appealing thing to dive into if you long for the feel of earth on your fingers and watching things grow. Providing some of your own food reduces costs and packaging waste and ensures that others have access to healthy foods.

- HAVE LAGOM MEETINGS. Sit down with your friends, family, and neighbors and tell them about the lagom spirit. Brainstorm on how you as individuals and as a community can come up with new ways to put moderation into practice. Somebody will almost certainly come up with an idea you've never thought of!

Lagom is never about being austere or stoic, either at home or in the world. If the whole point is to be happier and more fulfilled, how would that work if we deny ourselves life's simple pleasures? On the other hand, too much of anything, good or bad, can leave us feeling unbalanced, even discontent. By adopting a middle way, we can be ready to enjoy the good things that bring us joy. The following chapters will discuss those many good things in more detail.

CHAPTER 2

Friluftsliv

Connection to Nature by Being in Nature

(PRONOUNCED "FREE-LOOFTS-LIV")

NORWAY

“There is no bad weather, only bad clothing.”

—NORWEGIAN PROVERB

Friluftsliv literally means "free-air-life," a lovely word and concept invented by the Norwegian poet Henrik Ibsen (1828–1906) back in 1871. It comes from his 1859 poem "On the Heights," which tells of a young farmer who goes into the wilderness to clear his head and feel free:

> *Here in this deserted dwelling*
> *I have housed my wealth of treasure;*
> *There's a bench, a stove, sweet smelling*
> *Air* [friluftsliv], *and time to think at leisure.*

Ibsen intended friluftsliv to mean the fulfillment that one gets from being in nature. Not by doing anything specific, such as playing sports, hiking, rock climbing, etc., but just by being out in the greater wild world, by being in the moment and the place. This one-on-one experience of the natural world is a true food for the soul.

There's no doubt that many of us who live in urban environments feel increasingly restless and cut off from our origins in nature. We have millions of years of evolution behind us where we lived in close contact with the natural world, and now locking ourselves away in concrete buildings under artificial light is not only a mistake, but also it's been proven in countless studies to be unhealthy, both for the mind and body. Norwegians refer to connecting to the natural world as *naturrensing*, or "nature cleansing."

Clearly, it's good to get out, but what does that mean, and what do you do? It's important to realize that being outdoors does not have to mean doing outdoorsy things. So, if you're afraid that you'll have to invest in expensive hiking equipment, a tent, ice picks, or whatever, you can lay those fears to rest. Unless you actually *want* to do any of those things, of course! Remember that partaking of friluftsliv is much more about *being* than *doing*. The whole point is to slow down and get out of your head, get out of the compulsive need to be doing something, to be going somewhere, to be achieving something. With friluftsliv, the journey is the destination.

You don't need to worry about living near a large natural resource. Taking a walk in your local park or even sitting in your backyard on a summer afternoon listening to the wind and the birds are both fine examples of losing yourself in nature this way. The point is to reconnect with your natural surroundings by experiencing them directly, not thinking about them, not reading about them, and not looking at pretty pictures on the internet! You can experience this on your own or with friends and family, but remember, if you bring others along, the point is not to get caught up in distractions. It will do you no good to go for a forest walk if your friend is going to spend the entire time talking about office politics. The whole idea is to shut that all off and experience the world around you. Try keeping as silent as you can and let the natural world speak to you for a change.

Numerous studies have shown the beneficial effects of being out in nature. It can energize us, lower rates of depression, reduce cortisol levels, and strengthen our immune systems. Just twenty minutes a day in the "real" world can significantly improve our feelings of happiness. We lived as a part of this world for untold millennia, only to decide in the last 100 years that we don't need it anymore! That's proving to be a huge mistake.

A Stanford University study from 2015 reported that over 50 percent of the world's people now live in urban areas, and that urbanization is associated with rising rates of mental illness and stress. It seems that it's not just a nice thing to do; we *need* to get back to nature. The study recommended making sure that people in urban areas still have access to the natural world, even if only in the form of parks and other green spaces. Our well-being seems to depend on it!

In Norway, the home of friluftsliv, there is national support for the need to be outdoors. In 1957, the Norwegian government passed the Outdoor Recreation Act, which gives its people a "right to roam," as long as they follow certain guidelines and are respectful of property and the land itself. In real terms, the right of access to land had been established for centuries (some say back to Viking times), but it was finally enshrined into law with this act. It is a right that Norwegians hold very dear and make use of at every opportunity! While for many, this right means epic hikes and outdoor adventure sports, for others, it really is a chance to commune with nature in Norway's spectacular countryside and feel revived and refreshed.

It's important to remember that being in nature, as great as it is, is not a substitute for medical or mental-health care. If you are concerned about any condition, always speak with your doctor or mental-health-care professional. Experiencing nature should never replace your own health program, but it can be a wonderful supplement to it.

If you would like to experience friluftsliv for yourself, this chapter will give you a plan to get started. Remember that this is not about conquering something new, exercising in the classic sense of the word, or trying to go somewhere grand and remote. It's also important not to get overwhelmed and think that you must keep to a complex schedule or routine. This is about experiencing nature directly and letting it wash over you. If you can do this, you'll feel a sense of renewal and gratitude.

SO WHAT DO YOU ACTUALLY *DO*?

Getting back to nature may sound great, but you're probably wondering what you do when you get there. And that's the beauty of friluftsliv: you don't have to *do* anything if you don't want to! The concept of being outdoors can encompass just about anything you can imagine while you're there. In fact, it might even be better to do as little as possible.

Friluftsliv is really more about achieving a state of mind and being than going out and doing ambitious things. If you can get out somewhere, take the time to just appreciate being there, being in the moment.

Silence the distractions on your phone and in your head and take it all in. This may seem easy, but many people find it very hard to just shut down and "be" for a while. Studies have shown that even sitting quietly for a while (with the promise of a small cash reward if they succeeded) proved to be very difficult for some people. If your mind is go-go-go all the time, you may find that doing nothing takes a little getting used to. At the end of this chapter, there some simple meditation practices you can use to try to bring yourself into a better state of calm.

But the important thing to remember is just to take the time, wherever you are, to appreciate your natural surroundings and become more mindful of them. Admiring an impressive tree or literally stopping and smelling the roses can do wonders for your mental and emotional state over time.

Douglas LaBier, PhD, writes that "a new empirical study [from a University of British Columbia Study] finds evidence in support of what we see clinically. It found that virtually any form of immersion in the natural world, outside of your internal world, heightens your overall well-being and well as more positive engagement with the larger human community."

In that same study, Holli-Anne Passmore noted that the findings strongly suggest that simply taking the time to notice the natural things already around us can have a dramatic effect on our health and well-being. "This wasn't about spending hours outdoors or going for long walks in the wilderness," she wrote. "This is about the tree at a bus stop in the middle of a city and the positive effect that one tree can have on people."

Think about that for a minute. This study showed that you don't have to have access to a vast wilderness to feel better. Even taking in small amounts of natural objects on a regular basis around you can lift your mood and improve your outlook. With that in mind, it makes it much easier to make a plan to get the most out of the time you actually have. You'll be able to get more of the natural world into your life in a way that works for you.

A PLAN TO GET BACK TO NATURE

So you want to get outside more. Fantastic! But what does that actually mean? Well, you're going to have a decision to make. It's not enough to just think about getting outdoors. If you want to do it, you have to make the commitment to doing it! With so many things in our lives, we often dream about doing them, but never get around to it. This is especially true when it comes to exercising more, going to a gym, committing to eating more healthfully, and so on. We all know about starting a new fitness routine: we begin with great enthusiasm only to fizzle out a week or two later and give up on it. All that initial excitement just seems to evaporate in a matter of days, and we're right back where we started. Admit it, you've done it, and so has everyone else! The sad fact is that good intentions often aren't enough.

So, it's reasonable to assume that if you're going to choose to get out more, you'll need to come up with a plan to do it. Happily, this plan can be quite simple and doesn't require a lot of complex forethought.

If after thinking about getting out, it still doesn't seem possible, ask yourself why. There are no bad answers to this, and you should never feel guilty about having objections. There could be any number of reasons that are holding you back, but fortunately, there are simple solutions for each concern:

- TIME: It's easy to just say "get out more," or "do it after work," but the reality is that many people work very long hours and are exhausted at the end of the day. The last thing they want to do is go foraging through the woods, or even go sit in the local park, especially after sunset! In the age of Covid-19 and more people working at home, the prospect of getting out can seem daunting, even if we have a few more hours back because we're not commuting to work. If we're trying to maintain social distancing, going to a place with other people may not seem very appealing. Fortunately, you don't need to spend a lot of time. Even just fifteen minutes is enough, and it might be nothing more than a quick walk around the neighborhood.

- LOCATION: Depending on where you live, it may be difficult for you to have any access to the natural world at all. This is a terrible problem for many people, and it presents a real barrier to getting out into nature, one that shouldn't be dismissed or ignored. But remember the UBC study: even taking a little time to observe and admire the trees or flowers in your neighborhood can be very helpful.

- RESPONSIBILITIES: We all have various responsibilities that tug at us every day. Again, even if someone works at home, they may also be looking after children, being responsible for their care and education. Or someone may have an elderly parent to care for. There are countless reasons why you might not be able to just pick up and go for a walk, even for ten minutes. This is a legitimate concern that needs to be considered. Can you take a few minutes to step out the door and breathe some fresh air? Take a walk to the end of the block and back? Every little bit helps!

- PERSONAL HEALTH AND ENERGY: Many people are just not in the condition to get out for outdoor trips; some may even be housebound. At the very least, you may be worn out after a long workday and in no mood to go anywhere. This is perfectly understandable and reasonable. Think about how you can bring nature to you. Would a few low-maintenance houseplants or flowers spruce up your home a little? Studies have shown that being around even a little greenery can boost our moods.

- LACK OF INTEREST: Maybe the idea of getting outside just isn't that appealing to you. You're a homebody, you like your comforts to be inside, and spending time outdoors when you don't have to just isn't for you. There's nothing weird about you if this is the case, by the way! But it can be fun to get outside your comfort zone a little. Often, we resist trying new things until we actually do it, and then wonder why we resisted! Commit to stepping outside, even just for a few minutes, several times in the coming week.

The good news is that if any of these reasons sound familiar to you, you're not alone, and none of them have to interfere with you getting an occasional gulp of good fresh air! Always remember that friluftsliv really isn't about going on epic hikes at the weekends, conquering the wilderness, indulging in extreme sports, or anything else high energy and dangerous (though you can certainly do all those things, if you want to). It can just be about taking a few minutes to get a change of pace and enjoy some silence and solitude in natural surroundings. It can be a time not to do anything, but to recharge. Can you manage a little outside time once a week? Once every two weeks? Then you already have an "in" to take advantage of this practice! The next sections will show you how.

MAKE THE TIME

Making some time to indulge in a little friluftsliv doesn't require eating up huge chunks of your available hours. Far from it, in fact. It really is up to you how much time you want to put into your natural experience. If you can only afford thirty minutes once a week, that's a perfectly good place to start. Let's say that you decide you can spare thirty minutes three times a week to get outside more. What will you do with that time?

You'll obviously have to work your outdoors time into your schedule and what you can realistically do. Will that time be early in the morning, or later in the afternoon or evening? Can you do it on a lunch break? What are the best hours for you? Do you like to get an early start, or do you dread the idea of morning until you've had your coffee? Maybe you come alive after sunset. Understanding your own personal clock and how that can fit into your friluftsliv time is important.

If you're a morning person, just how much of a morning person are you? Can you get up an extra half hour early and work twenty minutes of friluftsliv time into your life a few days a week? The peace and quiet of the dawn hours might be perfect, if you're already an early riser. But if mornings make you cringe and you have a day job, can you put aside a little time on weekends, and/or later in the day? Is there a comfortable and safe place you can go after sunset for a bit? Remember, you don't need to go trudging off to the wilds, or even a local park. Even sitting in your backyard after sunset, taking in your surroundings, can be a great way to soak up some natural goodness.

The point is not the quantity, but rather the quality. If you can only afford twenty minutes every Sunday morning or evening, that's a good place to start, if you can keep at it. It's what you do with that time that's important.

The citizens of Sommarøy, on an island off the coast of northern Norway, launched a drive in 2019 to declare their island a time-free zone, the world's first! They argue that since time has no meaning in summer or winter (either never-ending day or night, respectively), they should not be constrained by the demands of imposed time. Maybe they're on to something?

CHOOSE YOUR LOCATION

As noted, you don't need to be trudging out on day-long outdoor adventures, though that's fine if you want to and can! Do you have a nice park nearby? Even just a small park with grass and trees, one that's a little bit on the quiet side, would be a perfect choice. In Norway's capitol city, Oslo, it's estimated that 95 percent of its residents have a park or open space within 1,000 feet of their home, which is an amazing thought. Many of us are not so lucky, but that doesn't mean we can't find opportunities to appreciate open space. Here are some ideas.

- If there are no parks nearby or you can't get out to one on a regular basis, think closer to home. Do you have a backyard of some kind, even a small one, where you can sit and reconnect with the natural world for a bit? This seems increasingly to be a luxury for many people, so please do take advantage of it if you do have this kind of space!

- Maybe just try a quick walk around the block of your own neighborhood. Take some time to see what's there. Are there impressive trees, bushes, mosses, or flower arrangements? Do a quick reconnaissance over a block or two and really pay attention. What do you see that you might have missed before? There are probably all sorts of things you've never noticed.

- If you do go to a local park, try to go when there are fewer people; yes, that's easier said than done! If it's not possible to be alone, at least try to locate a part of the park that's not overrun with people; you need to try to have a little space to yourself. Again, on your first trip, take the time to notice things you might not have seen before. What kinds of trees are there? What kinds of flowers? How large is the space? Are there any outdoor aromas you notice while you're there? The point is to get yourself back in touch with your surroundings in an immediate way. The meditation at the end of this chapter will help more with this process.

- If you do have the chance to get out somewhere more remote, make use of these same activities to get yourself better attuned to the area. You don't want to get lost in the wilderness, so it's good to get a bit more familiar with the territory. Do you need a map? Do you need to bring anything with you? Having some water and snacks is always a good idea if you're going to be out for more than an hour or two. Just remember that the main point is not to go on an adventure hike, though you could do that after you've experienced your oneness with nature, if you want!

DON'T GET TOO AMBITIOUS

It's important to remember that friluftsliv is not a competitive sport. There has been some concern recently that some Norwegian outdoor sporting associations are advertising their activities as a way to indulge in friluftsliv, when nothing could be further from the truth. Rock climbing or snowboarding will certainly get you outside, and likely give you a new appreciation for nature, but it's not the same kind of appreciation that friluftsliv strives for.

The good news is that you can do exactly what you feel you need to do for yourself at the time. Maybe one week you will feel like taking a longer walk, while the next, you can't bear the idea. That's just fine. We all have our ups and downs and go through all kinds of cycles and stages of health, so do what you can when you can. Maybe you want to do a small venture out most times but want to try out a longer walk or something different once a month. If you can, this is a great way to add a bit of variety and keep your practice interesting. But if you can't or don't want to, that's OK, too. You control the pace and the content of your friluftsliv experience, and you can tailor it exactly to what you want and need.

There's no need to get ambitious on your first few times out, or even your first fifty times out. Figure out what works best for you and stick with that for a while. Developing a "friluftsliv routine" might be just the thing to help you stick with it. Everyone has their own level of physical abilities and tolerance, and what might work for one person will not be right for someone else.

Another big concern? That little thing called the weather. Being at one with nature may sound like a blast on a spring day or an autumn afternoon, but in the heat of the summer or the freezing cold of winter, it might be the last thing you want to do! Whatever your goals are for experiencing friluftsliv, you are not obligated to slog through the snow to get to your local park, or wilt in the heat to sit under a tree. Be practical and realistic. The thought of taking a leisurely walk in a winter wood might be exhilarating for some, but sheer drudgery for others. Only you know what you prefer, and if a blizzard is blowing or the temperature is bursting the thermometer, you're fully entitled to give it a miss. You might try cultivating some indoor plants, or taking just a short walk around your neighborhood.

Remember the quote at the beginning of the chapter, though; it's all about how you dress. Norwegians often revel in experiencing the weather, whatever it is! Give yourself the "gift" of trying an outdoor excursion in less perfect weather, even if just once. If you're up for getting outdoors at less-than-ideal times of year, even for a bit, it can be a very interesting exercise to note how the plants and scenery change through the seasons. This is something we have mostly lost touch with, but it can be a great way to reconnect to the world and become more appreciative of what's right in front of you.

DITCH THE CELL PHONE AND OTHER DISTRACTIONS!

This can't be emphasized enough; it really can't. The whole point of getting away, even for a quarter of an hour, is to leave the cares of everyday life behind and disconnect. Sure, you may need to keep your phone with you, but turn it off, mute it, stuff it in a sack, whatever you need to do. The internet and incoming texts will keep for a little while, honest!

Often, people find that when they do unplug for a bit, they don't miss it nearly as much as they thought they would. Start small and work your way up. If you can only bear being offline for ten minutes at a time, work with that. Maybe in a week, you can try fifteen or twenty.

So much of the outdoor experience in Norway is about being outdoors and doing outdoor things. Hiking, skiing, kayaking, fishing, and foraging are by default outdoor things; texting is not, and chatting on the phone is not. Norwegians avidly look forward to experiences they can only have outside, so be more like them.

Bringing along other people may seem like a good idea: having a buddy along can keep you both committed to a regular outdoor-time schedule, just as it would if you were going to a yoga class, the gym, etc. But as far as friluftsliv is concerned, this is not always the best thing to do. Think about it: almost always, you're going to be chatting about things on your way there, and that conversation will spill over into your outdoor walk or park visit. Or you'll be sitting quietly, and one or the other will say something, and the next thing you know, you're immersed in a full-blown conversation, and ignoring the whole reason you're even out there. It happens all the time.

So, even if you're an extrovert and love doing things with friends and groups, consider trying this practice on your own for a while at the beginning. See how it goes. Do you get antsy about being alone and silent for any more than a few minutes? Some people are just wired that way, and there's nothing wrong with it. But learning to value a little bit of peace and quiet will do you no harm! It will give you the chance to immerse yourself in your surroundings and get the most out of the experience. Once you're out there, make the commitment to really be out there, and go with that! Maybe you'll be pleasantly surprised. After you've gotten a bit more used to this, you can start including others in your outdoor activities.

We'll end this chapter with a few simple meditation exercises that can clear your head and bring you into better focus to experience the natural world. If you want to try to take it all in, it helps to be in the right state of body and mind.

MEDITATION AND MORE: WAYS TO BE RATHER THAN DO

When people think of "meditation," they often think of gurus sitting for hours on end, showing tremendous amounts of discipline with the goal of achieving lofty spiritual aims. That's certainly one kind, but for the purposes of this book, these are more like simple claiming and breathing exercises to get you in the mood for your outdoor experience, wherever you are. These are best done when you can be undisturbed for a few minutes, so that may influence when and where you can do them. If it's not possible to do them in the place you've chosen to go to, then you might have to set them aside for now or try to find another location where you can make use of them. In fact, the first of these exercises can be done at home if you can't perform it outside.

SQUARE BREATHING EXERCISE

This is a very simple meditation to bring you to a place of calm. Once you get used to it, you'll be surprised at how quickly it can work. And you'll find that you can do it pretty much anywhere that you have a minute or two: at work, when waking up, when going to bed, etc. It's often called "square breathing" simply because it involves an even way of breathing in and out.

1. Close your eyes and take a few deep but gentle breaths. Become aware of your breath and the slow rising and falling of your chest and stomach as you inhale and exhale.

2. Take a breath in, and in your mind, do a slow count to four, until your lungs are full.

3. Hold this breath for a count of four, for the same amount of time as your in-breath.

4. Exhale, again for a count of four, until your lungs are empty.

5. Hold for another count of four.

6. Begin the exercise again. Repeat as many times as you wish, or as many as feels comfortable.

The point is to make your breathing into a "square" by having each of these four actions take the same amount of time. This exercise can have an amazing effect pretty quickly and bring you to feeling calm and relaxed. Over time, you may find that you can take deeper breaths and count to larger numbers, but four is a good number to start with, and will make the exercise pleasant rather than a chore. Don't think of it as a workout that you need to improve on—just let it be and develop in its own way.

AWARENESS OF ONE'S SPACE AND SURROUNDINGS

This is a great exercise promoted by Glasgow-based writer, social historian, and devotee of all things Norse, Ryan Smith. It allows you to get better in touch with the outdoors by tuning in specifically to certain surroundings. It's a great way to learn to be in nature and be in the moment.

1. Find a quiet place where you can be undisturbed for at least ten minutes. Yes, this is not always easy to do. You can choose to sit or stand as you wish. A park bench is fine, or maybe you want to stand near a large tree. Whatever works for you is great.

2. Begin by doing the square breathing exercise for a little while, as many repetitions as you feel comfortable doing. Three or four cycles should be enough to start.

3. Once you are calm, keep your eyes closed and open yourself to your surroundings by listening. Simply take in everything you hear, but mainly the natural sounds: the wind in trees, any nearby water, the sounds of birds, etc. It's entirely possible that a leaf blower will start up or a loud car will zoom by; just ignore those and bring yourself back to natural sounds, the ones that *really* matter.

4. After a minute or two of being with these sounds, try to understand their nature. Which one is loudest? Which is quietest? Which sound is nearest to you? Which sound is farthest away? Get a sense of these different sound volumes and locations, and their relation not only to you, but to each other. If a gust of wind blows all of a sudden, does it make the water in the creek less audible? If a bird calls out, does it draw your attention away from everything else? Sit with this for a minute or two and just observe.

5. Try to stay in the present moment. As most meditators have found, this is much easier said than done! You'll find almost immediately that your mind starts to wander, random thoughts pop up, and everything

seems to be conspiring to ruin your moment of peace! This is entirely normal. When it happens, just bring your attention back to the present, back to the sounds you are taking in. Each time your mind goes for an unplanned excursion, gently bring your attention back to the here and now. If you practice this regularly, it will get easier over time, and you'll find that your thoughts take fewer unwanted trips.

6. Stay with this state of being in the moment for as long as you feel comfortable. The first time, it may only be a minute or two; that's fine.

7. When you're ready, take a deep breath and open your eyes. You may find that you notice more because you've spent a little time taking it all in before looking at your surroundings. You may see the bird you heard chirping, or notice the babbling brook, or see tree branches flapping in the wind. It may even feel more *real* to you.

You can also try this exercise by using a relaxed gaze. Try to notice all of the largest, smallest, nearest, and closest things to you, and how they change. A combination of both of these exercises is a great way to really tune in to your immediate environment.

The point of this exercise is to give you a greater feeling of connection to the world around you. If you practice it regularly, you will become more attuned to your natural surroundings, and more likely to hear the sounds around your own home that call to you through the chatter of modern life. Friluftsliv is about immersion in the natural world, and this simple meditation is a great way to immerse yourself. Don't be surprised if you become calmer and more aware as you progress over weeks and months of trying it. That's just what you want to do!

CHAPTER 3

Fika

Taking Daily Coffee Breaks and Other Comforting Rituals

(PRONOUNCED "FEE-KAH")

SWEDEN

“Seriousness and pleasure should thrive together.”

—SWEDISH PROVERB

Fika is a simple word that means something like "coffee break." But it doesn't have a good translation, and fika is much more than that. It's a whole component of Swedish society, but the idea behind it is simply that we should set aside time for a daily break and enjoy the good things in life. The classic coffee break in many other countries is often just a fifteen-minute stop in the workday to down some poorly made coffee (or possibly some good coffee from a local vendor for a high price), and maybe choke down a donut before rushing back to work, no doubt with a bit of indigestion. Coffee is used in the United States and elsewhere as fuel. It's meant to rev you up in the morning and get you firing on all cylinders to face the day's challenges. You might chug some more at 3:00 p.m. to get you through the rest of the day. But what if the humble coffee break could be more than that?

In Sweden, fika is a whole concept, a state of mind. Instead of giving you a boost to speed things up, it's all about slowing things down for a while and taking the time to savor a great cup of coffee (or whatever beverage you prefer), along with some sweet treats: pastry (*fikabröd*), cakes, cookies, cinnamon buns, sandwiches, whatever takes your fancy. It's said that people in Sweden are among the main consumers of coffees and cakes in the world, along with Finland. It's estimated that Swedes consume around eighteen pounds of coffee beans each per year! Fika is no doubt a big part of the reason.

True fika doesn't have to be enjoyed only in the afternoon; it can actually take place anytime throughout the day. It's most often shared with friends, and can be in a café, at home, at work, wherever you like. In fact, it's something you can take part in several times during the day, if you wish; imagine that! And while you can definitely set some time aside for a personal fika if you wish, making the effort to gather with friends and family is really what the whole thing is about.

Businesses in Sweden often have fika breaks, and not only because they are a welcome addition to the day. Studies have shown greater employee satisfaction and productivity in businesses that have made fika a key part of the workday, so it's obviously something that everyone should be doing! A fika at work may only be fifteen minutes long (or up to thirty), and may happen at, say, 10:00 a.m. and 3:00 p.m. A fika on your own time (say, at home) can last for as long as you want it to!

The word "fika" is actually a slang term for "coffee" that's been around since the nineteenth century. The Swedish word for coffee, *kaffi*, was inverted to *ffika*, and then *fika*, and there you have it! It's been a part of the language and culture ever since. In Sweden, the word is both a noun and a verb; you might say something like, "It was good to fika with you!"

How you actually enjoy fika is up to you, but it doesn't need to be elaborate. Treats are best if they're homemade, but you don't need to worry about preparing a feast every day; a few nibbles is fine, and it's also OK to buy something you like at a bakery or store. There is no one correct way to fika. The point should be to recognize it as a time to unplug and slow down. Many people enjoy lighting candles to go with their little coffee ritual. Dim the lights and light a candle or two, sit down at a table with friends, and enjoy some good coffee, some good conversation, and a sweet snack. Enjoy each other's company and talk about things that are not work-related. Get out of the daily grind and appreciate taking a little time for the things that are really important.

If you would like to bring fika into your life, here are some ideas and recipes to make it happen! You don't need to be an expert baker or a master barista to get the most out of this little break. If coffee is not your thing, you can have tea, or whatever beverage you like. The point is to indulge a little in something you enjoy, and to do it with others when you can.

SET THE SCENE FOR FIKA

Happily, fika can be as simple or as elaborate as you want it to be, or have the ability make it. Is it just a nice drink and a sweet nibble? That's fine! Do you sometimes want to go all out and make luxury drinks and cakes or other food to go with it? That's great, too! The real point of fika is to take a break, enjoy the moment, and treat yourself a little, no matter how small that treat is. There's no need to break the bank and spend large amounts of time making elaborate snack presentations. Here are some ideas for how to make manageable and fun preparations for your break.

- **TAKE THE TIME:** The most basic thing you need to do is set aside the time, whatever time you can. If you're at home, you'll probably have a little more flexibility with your day, and you might be able to fika for a bit longer. At work, you'll probably be on a schedule, and only get a certain number of minutes. Either way, try to have your fika at about the same time every day, whether in the morning, afternoon, or both. It will become a part of your routine that you'll look forward to.

- FIKA AT WORK: Work-time fikas need to be practical as well as enjoyable. The standard American coffee break can be transformed into a fika experience with a little creativity. Is there a new coffee shop nearby you've been wanting to try out? Make that your fika destination and go one day a week to start. Invite a friend and take a few minutes to get out of the work scene. Spend that time talking about anything but work; the point is to get away from it, so ban work topics from the conversation!

- FIKA WHEN WORKING AT HOME: Even before Covid-19, many people did their work at home. If you're one of them, this gives you more freedom and flexibility to have a break when it suits you. But the point of fika is the same: take a break. If you get up from your computer, don't automatically go check your phone or dive into social media. Take twenty minutes or a half hour and disconnect. If you get in the habit of doing this at the same time every day, it'll be something to look forward to!

- FIKA AT HOME: When you're at home and not working, you may have the option to make your fika a bit more elaborate, especially if you are inviting friends over, or spending time with your family. Of course, it doesn't have to be fancy; the point is to enjoy your break, no matter what foods you have. But once in a while, it's fun to splurge and make a fika that's a bit more ambitious. The recipes in this chapter will give you some good ideas for places to start.

- FIKA IN OTHER PLACES: There's no reason you can't enjoy your break somewhere else, too, if you have the time and the means. You might want to go to a beautiful park, where you can bring your fine coffee in a thermos and your snack in a plastic container. Or maybe you have a chance to sit by the sea and take in the sounds of the waves. What matters is that you're enjoying it and getting away for a little bit. Be creative.

- BE IN THE MOMENT: Regardless of whether you're at work or at home, use your fika break as a chance to actually have a break. Forget about work and life's other cares. Just for a few minutes, focus on the delicious beverage and the tasty sweet you have. Smell your coffee or tea before sipping, appreciate the texture of your cake or cookie, get in touch with those sensory experiences, and remind yourself just how amazing it is to be able to smell and taste.

- SET THE MOOD: You might be somewhat limited at work (or maybe not!), but at home, you're free to do whatever else you like that helps you unwind for a few minutes. Play some of your favorite music (though death metal may not relax you all that much!), maybe light a candle or two, draw the curtains, or open them wide, whatever takes your fancy. Use your best coffee mug and your best dishes to set out your cake or snacks. Create a space for yourself in the security of your own home and enjoy those minutes that are just for you and your companions.

- ENJOY THE TIME: Whether in a café or other setting, at home, a park, or wherever you prefer to go, remember that this is a time to step back and appreciate simple pleasures that we all too often take for granted. If you've invited a friend, take the time to catch up a little, find out what they're up to, and share your own stories. And speaking of inviting others, a fika break at a café can also be a great first date. It's low pressure, doesn't last too long (which may leave you both wanting more!), and who doesn't love good drinks and food? Telling your date about the practice of fika and why you do it is a great conversation starter, too!

COFFEE: THE ESSENCE OF FIKA

Coffee was probably introduced to Sweden from trade with the Ottoman Empire in the sixteenth century. But you might be surprised to learn that it wasn't very popular at first, at least not with the king, who saw it as a danger to public order and well-behaved citizens (all that caffeine!). Coffee was heavily taxed or even banned to discourage people from drinking it, but its popularity grew over the centuries, until it was fully legalized in the early 1800s. And coffee drinkers have never looked back!

These days, we pretty much take coffee for granted. Arguably, it's the drink that runs the world, so the idea of using it as a way to slow down seems more than a little subversive. And that only makes fika more satisfying! Of course, some people have issues with caffeine and can't drink it. That's no problem; there are many outstanding decaffeinated coffees that can be used as substitutes in these recipes, whether you're using a coffee pot, a drip, pods, an espresso machine, or any other method. Or, maybe you just don't like coffee. Believe it or not, that's OK, too! You can drink tea or whatever other beverage you prefer. The whole point is to enjoy the experience! There are recipes for other drinks in this chapter, in case you're not into coffee, or maybe just want to try something different once in a while.

But assuming that coffee is your drink of choice, here are a few recipes that go beyond everyday coffee and offer a little more in taste and sensation. Your regular coffee is just fine, of course, but here are some new ideas to add a little variety to your everyday drink. Whether you revel in the full-on jolt or need decaf, you can use these recipes to spice up your fika and lift things up from the ordinary. You can enjoy your coffee in the way you usually make it: drip filter, French press, coffee maker, pod machine, Chemex, even instant.

CARDAMOM SPICED COFFEE

Originating in India, cardamom is one of the most popular spices in Sweden, especially in baked goods. But it works equally well in coffee. Various cultures (Turkish, Ethiopian, Indian) have enjoyed cardamom in their coffee for centuries, and it makes a lovely addition to any cup! Cardamom coffee can be made in whatever way you prefer to make coffee.

Some tips:

> *If you grind your own beans, crush open 2–4 cardamom pods (to taste), and remove the seeds inside. Discard the pods. Add these seeds to the beans before grinding; alternately, add up to ⅔ teaspoon ground cardamom to the mix, especially if you buy pre-ground coffee. Use pour over, French press, drip, or whatever method you prefer.*

You may need to adjust the amount of cardamom to taste the first few times; a good place to start is 1 pod per cup to be served. Cardamom can disappear a bit into the stronger coffee flavor, so keep that in mind, and add more as you need and like.

CINNAMON SPICED COFFEE

Cinnamon is another Indian spice that works well in almost any hot drink: coffee, tea, cider, etc. It's spicy, warming, sweet, and surprisingly good for you! Try adding some to your coffee for a spicy twist on your usual cup.

You can add 1–2 teaspoons of ground cinnamon to 2 cups of coffee beans or 10 tablespoons of ground coffee and prepare as usual, adjusting for taste, with 1–2 teaspoons per pot of coffee made.

Alternately, you can set a cinnamon stick in your coffee mug and just let it sit, giving you a nice, subtle warming flavor!

MOCHA COFFEE

Chocolate and coffee, who doesn't love it? Maybe a few people don't, but if it sounds good to you, then here is a simple recipe for blending these two classic flavors together. Make your fika an extra treat once in a while!

The simplest way to make this recipe is just to stir a tablespoon of unsweetened cocoa powder into your mug of freshly brewed coffee. Add sweeteners or not as you like, and you're good to go!

OTHER COFFEE BLENDS

Have fun trying out these other ingredients to jazz up your coffee. Try alone, or mix and match and see what you like best.

VANILLA COFFEE: Add 1 teaspoon of vanilla extract per cup. Add to the grounds before brewing.

BOURBON COFFEE: Add bourbon (or another spirit, such as rum) to taste, if you want to live a little!

NUTMEG COFFEE: Sprinkle a little nutmeg on top of your coffee in the mug.

SECRETLY SALTED COFFEE: Strangely enough, a pinch of salt can neutralize a bit of the coffee's bitterness. Add ⅛ of a teaspoon (or less) to your ground coffee before brewing.

TEATIME IS FIKA TIME

Does coffee make you cringe? Is tea your thing? Is it too hot to drink either of them? No problem! There are plenty of alternatives to coffee when you're enjoying fika. Tea is an obvious substitute, but you can also enjoy other hot drinks, or even cold drinks, as you'll see in the next section. Whatever makes you happy and comforted is what will make fika work for you. In this section, we'll look at a few tea recipes that go beyond the usual, and then a few other drinks that you might like to try. Again, if caffeine is your enemy, decaf tea and herbal teas are just fine (there's an herbal tea recipe later on).

SPICY CHAI

Chai is an Indian classic, usually combining black tea, cinnamon, ginger, cardamom, cloves, black pepper, and other goodies into a heavenly mix that delights the senses and warms the body. Its spicy flavors warm on a winter day and go beautifully with fika treats. While there are many great varieties that you can buy, it's fun to brew it up yourself and let the aromas fill your home. This tea can either have caffeine or not, as you prefer, and it can be made with hot milk (traditional), hot water, or a milk substitute. Use this basic recipe as a place to start and vary it as you wish.

MAKES 1 CUP

1–2 whole cinnamon sticks

5–8 green cardamom pods

1 teaspoon whole black peppercorns

3–4 whole cloves

1–2 star anise pods (optional)

2–3 whole allspice berries, or ¼ teaspoon ground (optional)

2–3 fresh mint leaves, torn (optional)

2 tablespoons ginger root, grated or sliced, or ½ teaspoon ground ginger

3 tablespoons loose leaf black tea, or 3–4 black tea bags*

2 cups milk, dairy or plant-based**

Sweetener to taste, if desired

**You can substitute decaffeinated tea for regular tea.*

***Almond milk, oat milk, and soy milk are all good substitutes for dairy.*

1. Add the cinnamon stick(s), cardamom pods, peppercorns, and cloves, as well as star anise, allspice berries, and mint leaves (if desired), to the bowl of a mortar (or cutting board), and use pestle (or heavy pan) to crush a little. They don't need to be turned to powder. Just break them up enough to help release their flavor.

2. In a medium saucepan, add the crushed spices, 2½ cups water, and grated (or sliced or ground) ginger and bring

to a boil over high heat. Then reduce heat to medium-low and simmer for about 15 minutes, or until the mixture reduces by about one-third.

3. Add tea and milk, and reduce heat to low. Cover and continue to simmer for 5 minutes to let the flavors blend.

4. Then turn off heat and, still covered, let steep for 5 minutes more or longer for deeper flavor.

5. Add sweetener of choice to taste (if desired) and strain through a fine mesh strainer into a teacup. Keep strained, cooled leftovers covered in the fridge up to 3 days.

Chai is enjoyed daily in India as an essential part of everyday life. It's served in homes, restaurants, and at countless chai stands on streets and roadsides. Some of these small servers date back generations, passed down through the family. Like fika, chai drinking has become a daily requirement for many!

VANILLA TEA

Vanilla is a lovely flavor to combine with black tea or most herbal teas. This makes a great morning tea, or a pleasant afternoon diversion.

The simplest way to enjoy this tea is just to add ½ teaspoon to your mug after you finish steeping your tea bag, tea ball, or however you prefer to make tea. Alternately, you can buy vanilla beans, scrape the pods, and cut them into small pieces. Add them to a tin with your loose tea of choice and use the tea as you normally would. Use 3–4 beans per cup of dried loose tea. Vanilla sugar is a good alternative; add to taste.

LEMON, GINGER, AND HONEY TEA

If you're in the mood for something without the obvious tea flavor, this recipe may be just the thing. Enjoy it hot in the winter or cold in the summer, for an invigorating and delightful drink that should go with just about anything you want to serve with it.

MAKES 1 CUP

One 1-inch piece fresh ginger root, grated or sliced

1 tablespoon lemon juice

Honey, to taste

Dash of whiskey, to taste (optional)

1. Add the grated ginger to a small teapot or a large mug. Pour over one cup of boiling water boiled water and let steep for 4–5 minutes. Add lemon juice. Strain the ginger tea as you pour it into the mug.

2. Stir in honey and the optional whiskey to taste.

With a touch of whiskey, this recipe resembles the classic hot toddy, and is especially nice on a cold winter evening, or when you're sick. Of course, this is entirely optional!

ENJOYING FIKA WITH OTHER BEVERAGES

Coffee and tea are the most popular beverages for the classic fika, but you're not bound by some law to stick to them. If you prefer something else, by all means, have it! Here are a few ideas for other kinds of drinks that can go just as well with your fika experience.

HOT APPLE CIDER

While in Britain, cider refers to an alcoholic drink made from apples, in the United States, the word usually refers to a sweet, spicy apple juice that is perfect for the autumn and winter months. It's a lovely alternative to coffee and tea, and while it is perfectly drinkable right out of the bottle, it's also great to spice it up just a bit more! It's served both hot and cold, but since fika leans toward the cozy, a satisfying hot mug of cider is just what's called for!

Many American ciders come pre-spiced and ready to drink. But it's better to find a plainer variety and spice it yourself. Apple juice works just fine, too. You can make as much or as little as you like at one time, just adjust the amounts given here accordingly.

MAKES 8 CUPS

8 cups apple cider or juice

2 cinnamon sticks or 2–3 teaspoons ground cinnamon

1 teaspoon whole allspice

1–2 teaspoons ground cloves

⅛–¼ teaspoon ground nutmeg

¼ cup packed brown sugar, or to taste

1 teaspoon vanilla extract (optional)

Bourbon or other spirit to taste (optional)

Extra cinnamon sticks for garnish (optional)

1. In a large pot over a medium to medium-low heat, add the cider or juice, spices, and sugar. Stir occasionally until the sugar has dissolved.
2. Cover and simmer for 10–15 minutes, stirring occasionally. Strain into mugs and serve, garnished with extra cinnamon sticks and a dash of bourbon or your favorite spirit (if desired).

GLÖGG

Glögg is a Swedish holiday tradition. Versions of it exist in other Nordic countries as well, and it is most welcome in the cold months. Because it's normally alcoholic, you might want to wait to have this drink until late afternoon, or on days when you're not going anywhere! It tends to be a mulled wine that's fortified with spirits and seasoned with spices and dried fruit—yum! As you can imagine, there are as many different recipes for it as there are people who make it, so if this one doesn't quite work for you, feel free to modify it or look at others. This drink is best enjoyed in the cold, dark seasons, but if you're feeling daring, there's no reason that you can't make a nice batch for a cool spring evening!

MAKES 5-6 CUPS

1 bottle dry red wine

1 cup brandy or bourbon

½–1 bottle ruby port

½ cup raisins, such as Thompson Seedless

2-inch piece of fresh ginger, thinly sliced

3–4 cardamom pods, cracked open

1–2 cinnamon sticks

8–10 whole cloves

1 orange, sliced into quarters, peel left on

½ cup sugar, or to taste

1. In a large stockpot over medium heat, heat the wine until it begins to simmer. Add the spirits and port and bring to a simmer again. Stir in raisins, ginger, cardamom, and cinnamon.

2. Stick 2–3 whole cloves into the peel of each orange slice. You can place them in decorative patterns, if you like. Add the clove-decorated orange slices to the wine.

3. Simmer on low for 20–30 minutes to let the spices and flavors blend. Do not let it boil. Add sugar to taste and let it dissolve completely. Simmer for a few more minutes. Strain through a cheesecloth and ladle into mugs to serve.

FIKA CAKES, COOKIES, AND MORE

Fika is not really fika without cakes or other goodies! The chance to have a nibble on something sweet and decadent is a highlight of the coffee break, and one that you'll no doubt enjoy greatly. There are an endless number of options when it comes to sweets, but one of the most popular in Sweden is some form of the cinnamon bun or roll, called *kanelbullar* in Swedish. These are popular at breakfast, lunch, afternoon, or anytime! Another popular option is a bun or cake made with cardamom, the *semla* (sweet roll) or *kardemummakaka* (cardamom cake). These treats were traditionally eaten around the time of Lent, but have been sneaking out into other times as well. Other treats—like apple buns and cakes, saffron buns (mainly during the winter holidays), and a chocolate cake—can all make perfect accompaniments to your fika experience. All of these go great with most beverages and add that lovely little something extra to your break time.

On the cookie side, you might like to try *spritzen* (Swedish butter cookies), gingersnaps, or Swedish chocolate cookies. Remember that you can make things as fancy or as simple as you want. While having home-baked goods is a lovely addition to the experience, if you only have time for a store-bought treat, that's fine. Just make sure that it's something you really enjoy.

CINNAMON BUNS (*KANELBULLAR*)

These classic Swedish delicacies are twisted into lovely, aromatic knotted buns, brushed with spiced sugar glaze, and crowned with a crystalline dusting of pearl sugar. They're lighter and much less messy than their rolled American cousins—no knife and fork required. And the average Swedish citizen polishes off more than three hundred of them per year!

MAKES 16 BUNS

FOR THE BUNS:

1 cup plus 2 tablespoons whole-fat milk, dairy or plant-based

2 ¼ teaspoons (1 package) active dry yeast

½ cup granulated sugar, divided

2 teaspoons ground cardamom

1 large egg, plus 1 egg yolk

2 teaspoons pure vanilla extract divided

2 teaspoons kosher salt, preferably Diamond Crystal

Between 3 and 4 cups unbleached all-purpose flour

4 tablespoons (½ stick) unsalted butter, at room temperature

Nonstick cooking spray

FOR THE FILLING:

4 tablespoons (½ stick) unsalted butter, at room temperature

½ cup packed dark brown sugar

5 teaspoons ground cinnamon

2 teaspoons ground cardamom

3 teaspoons vanilla bean paste

⅛ teaspoon kosher salt, preferably Diamond Crystal

FOR THE SPICED SIMPLE SYRUP GLAZE:

⅓ cup packed dark brown sugar

3 cardamom pods, split open (or ½ teaspoon ground cardamom)

One 3-inch cinnamon stick (or 2 teaspoons ground cinnamon)

1 vanilla bean split lengthwise (or 1 teaspoon vanilla bean paste)

FOR THE TOPPING:

¼ cup pearl sugar*

**Pearl sugar (also called "Swedish pearl sugar") is popular in Sweden. The sugar crystals have been compressed to form larger chunks that don't dissolve during baking, which makes it perfect for a topping! Added to these cookies, it looks like a dusting of snow. It is available in specialty stores and online.*

1. In a saucepan over high heat, warm milk to 115°F. Pour it into the bowl of a stand mixer fitted with the whisk attachment, and then add yeast and 1 teaspoon of the granulated sugar. Let stand until bubbling, about 10 minutes. Add the remaining granulated sugar, cardamom, egg, egg yolk, vanilla, and salt, and whisk to combine.

2. Switch to the dough hook, and gradually add 3 cups flour to the mixer bowl. Knead on slow and then medium-high speed just until the dough sticks to the hook. Add the remaining 1 cup flour as needed until a smooth dough comes together. Beat in butter. Turn out dough onto a flour-dusted work surface and, with flour-coated hands, shape it into a ball. Put dough ball into a cooking-spray-coated medium bowl, seam-side down, and cover. Put in a warm place to rise for at least 1 hour, or overnight in the fridge. Dough should double in size.

3. Prepare the filling by combining butter, brown sugar, cinnamon, cardamom, vanilla bean paste, and salt. Stir to combine.

4. Preheat oven to 350°F, and prepare a baking sheet by greasing with butter or lining with parchment paper. Place the risen dough on a work surface dusted with flour and flatten it with a flour-dusted rolling pin into an 18-by-12-inch rectangle. Spoon the filling mixture on top and spread it out evenly to the edges.

5. Along the longer side, mark the dough with a butter knife into three 6-inch segments. Use the marks as a guide to gently fold the dough into thirds so it's like a closed envelope. Rotate so the seam is in front and the open ends are to your right and left.

6. With a sharp knife parallel to the open ends, cut the dough envelope into sixteen ½-inch wide strips. To make the knotted shape, hold the end of one doubled strip between your first two fingers and thumb. Loop the tail over those first two fingers, all the way around them, and then tuck it under itself to make a knotted bun. (No need to stress; even the messiest knots bake up beautifully.) Place onto the prepared baking sheet. Repeat with the remaining strips. Cover, and let dough knots rise 45 minutes at room temperature.

7. For the spiced simple syrup glaze: In a saucepan over medium-high heat, combine brown sugar, ¼ cup water, cardamom, cinnamon, and vanilla. Bring to a boil, stirring constantly until sugar has dissolved; remove from heat.

8. With a pastry brush, cover the knots with spiced simple syrup. Sprinkle generously with pearl sugar. Bake for 18 minutes or until golden brown around the edges.

If you prefer American-style buns, simply roll the filling-covered dough into a log and slice it into rounds before baking. Any shape of cinnamon roll will give you the cinnamon and coffee experience that is such a beloved Swedish tradition. Or try swapping the amounts of cinnamon and cardamom for Swedish cardamom buns (*kardemummabullar*).

SWEDISH BUTTER COOKIES (*SPRITZ*)

These cookies are another holiday tradition in Sweden, though there's no reason why you can't enjoy them at other times of the year, of course! As with all of these recipes, there are many different versions, varying from region to region. Give these cookies a try when you're in the mood for something new and authentically Swedish. "Spritz" comes from the German "to squirt," and that's what you'll do with these, as you squirt the dough onto a baking sheet, with a piping bag or a cookie press. You can have fun trying out different shapes!

MAKES ABOUT 30 TO 35 COOKIES

FOR THE COOKIES:

1 cup unsalted butter, at room temperature

½ cup granulated sugar

2 large egg yolks

1 ½ teaspoon pure vanilla extract

2 cups all-purpose flour, sifted

¼ teaspoon kosher salt, preferably Diamond Crystal

FOR THE DECORATION:

Candied cherries, sprinkles, nuts, and tinted sugars, as desired

1. Preheat oven to 350°F. Grease two baking sheets and place them in the refrigerator while making the batter.

2. In the bowl of a stand mixer, beat the butter and sugar until light and fluffy, about 2 to 3 minutes. Add the egg

yolks and vanilla extract and beat until they are incorporated, scraping down the sides of the bowl as needed. Add the flour and salt and beat to combine.

3. Use a cookie press or a pastry bag fitted with a ½-inch-diameter open star tip. Fill the bag to about half full, twist the end to close, and, holding the bag perpendicular to the sheet, pipe stars, rosettes, or other patterns. The tip should almost touch the sheet. Space them about 2 inches apart.

4. Decorate with your garnishes in fun and festive patterns (if desired).

5. Bake for 12 to 14 minutes, or just until the edges are just browned. Remove from the oven and transfer the cookies to a wire rack to cool. These cookies will keep for about 10 days in a sealed container, or for several months if frozen.

SWEDISH CHOCOLATE COOKIES (*CHOKLADSNITTAR*)

Also known as chocolate cut cookies, these lovely, easy-to-make treats can add an authentically Swedish feel to your fika. Chocolaty and dusted with pearl sugar, they are a favorite childhood treat for many in Sweden, and they pair well with just about any drink. They are sliced horizontally into long, thin wedges that are great for dunking in drinks!

MAKES ABOUT 20 COOKIES

FOR THE COOKIES:

7 tablespoons unsalted butter

½ cup plus 1 tablespoon granulated sugar

1 cup plus 2 tablespoons unbleached all-purpose flour, or one-to-one gluten-free replacement

2 tablespoon unsweetened cocoa powder

½ teaspoon baking powder

½ teaspoon vanilla extract

1 large egg

FOR THE DECORATION:

1 large egg

¼ cup pearl sugar*

**Pearl sugar (also called "Swedish pearl sugar") is popular in Sweden. The sugar crystals have been compressed to form larger chunks that don't dissolve during baking, which makes it perfect for a topping! Added to these cookies, it looks like a dusting of snow. It is available in specialty stores and online.*

1. Preheat oven to 400°F and line a baking pan with parchment paper.
2. In the bowl of a stand mixer fitted with the paddle attachment, beat the butter and sugar until light and fluffy, about 2 to 3 minutes.
3. Add flour, cocoa powder, baking powder, vanilla, and egg, and beat until just combined into a soft dough.
4. Divide the dough into three equal parts on the parchment-lined baking sheet, and press each part with your hands until it is a long, flat rectangle, about ¼-inch thick.
5. Lay the sections out on your baking sheet. Leave some space in between them, since the dough will spread during baking.

6. Beat the second egg and brush it over the dough. Sprinkle each section with a generous portion of pearl sugar.

7. Bake for about 12 minutes. Check to see that the edges are hardening but the centers are still a bit soft.

8. Cut the cookies horizontally into 1-inch wide slices while they are warm. Leave the slices on the baking tray for another 10 minutes or so, until they have fully cooled. Transfer to a serving plate and enjoy with coffee, tea, or other drinks.

OTHER FIKA SNACK OPTIONS

In case you're wondering, fika doesn't have to be about sugary foods. In fact, there are many snacks that can be substituted, depending on your tastes and preferences. Plain fruit can be a nice accompaniment (especially in the summer months), and other snacks like finger sandwiches are entirely acceptable. The Swedish *smörgås*, or open-faced sandwich, is another cherished fika tradition. Use your imagination and indulge in what you want; it's the way of fika!

SWEDISH SANDWICHES (*SMÖRGÅSAR*)

If you'd prefer something a little less sweet to go with your fika, here's an alternative. Small sandwiches, called *smörgåsar* in Sweden, are a great pick-me-up in the mid-afternoon, just enough to hold you over between lunch and dinner, or a great prelunch snack to get you ready for the midday meal!

> *These are usually made with a thick crusty white bread or rye or pumpernickel bread, topped with butter and then whatever else you might like to put on it. Smoked salmon sandwiches* (laxsmörgåsar) *are a Nordic favorite. Other popular toppings include eggs and/or cheese, sliced radishes and other vegetables, and fresh herbs. Vegans could use hummus instead of butter. It's all about what will go with that coffee!*

For a party, layer good sandwich bread and fillings and decorate whimsically with sandwich fixings to make a Swedish sandwich cake, otherwise known as a *smörgåstårta*.

RYE CRACKERS TOPPED WITH ASSORTED GOODIES (*KNÄCKEBRÖD*)

Rye bread, rye crackers, and rye crispbread are another great Nordic tradition. They've been baked there for more than five hundred years. No wonder using crunchy crackers as a base for other foods is a satisfying fika snack.

Top these with gravlax, cured meats, hard cheeses, or whatever else you like, sweet or savory, and enjoy with your fika drink.

CHAPTER 4

Hygge

Coziness Brings Comfort, Courage, and Happiness

(PRONOUNCED "HOO-GUH")

DENMARK

"*Hygge* has been called everything from 'the art of creating intimacy,' 'coziness of the soul,' and 'the absence of annoyance,' to 'taking pleasure from the presence of soothing things,' 'cozy togetherness,' and my personal favorite, 'cocoa by candlelight.'"

—MEIK WIKING

Hygge seems to be all the rage these days; you've probably read articles about it, seen television news reports, seen a book or two in stores, or had someone recommend it to you. You may know that it comes from Denmark, and that Denmark is always ranked as one of the happiest places in the world, but beyond that, what is hygge? And what does it have to do with all those happy Danes? Scandinavia has very long, dark, and cold winters, and the idea of hygge seems a natural and welcome response. Indeed, a big part of the appeal of hygge is in creating your own personal space that's a refuge from the elements and the cares of the world.

As you can see in the preceding quote, hyyge is not really translatable into one word or idea. It's something that's felt rather than understood exactly, and it will mean different things to different people. It's about reveling in the cozy, the familiar, and the safe, about having a personal space to retreat to and cocoon—or having a few friends over for a great evening of good times and good company. It's about having a drink that you love at hand while you read a cherished book on the couch. It's about drinking wine with your partner while watching your favorite movie. It's about hearing a raging winter storm outside while sitting in front of a fire, as your favorite music plays in the background. It's about candles glowing and soft lights illuminating your home. It's about having a favorite nook to curl up in, or a favorite chair to sit on. It's about feeling the soft fur on your cat or dog as they sit with you and you pet them. It's about making your favorite food and serving it to the special people in your life.

Hyyge is all of these things and much more. See why it can't exactly be translated? But you probably also see why Denmark, the home of hygge, is so happy, even with its long winter nights and cold weather. Experiencing hygge brings warmth to one's life that no winter wind can chill and gives one a sense of security that no darkness can take away.

The good news is that hygge is not exclusive or expensive. In fact, the more rustic and homespun some things are, the better. It's not something that is only experienced at the holidays (though that is prime hygge time!), or something that you must set aside for only special times of the year. Hygge can and should be enjoyed all year round, and it's easy to get started!

Hygge is about creating the right atmosphere wherever you are (at home, at work, even in other places). It's about camaraderie and friendship; it's about feeling safe and being able to relax and let go of cares, even if just for a little while. Enjoy the moment. You don't have to necessarily *do* anything; just be comfortable enough to be yourself in a space that makes you comfortable.

THINGS THAT HYGGE REPRESENTS

Even if hygge doesn't have an exact one-word translation, there are several qualities about it that we all relate to and want more of in our lives. Here is a list of some of the things that should be on your mind when trying to immerse yourself in hygge and create a space for yourself and your loved ones.

- **CREATING THE RIGHT SETTING:** The way that your space is organized is central to the whole hygge experience. The lighting, the atmosphere, the mood, what you chose to put in the space, etc., will all enhance your hygge feelings and make your space inviting and desirable.
- **FEELING SAFE:** One of the main points of the hygge space is for it to be a little sanctuary from the cares of the world. So make sure that you can

feel safe where you are. It also means that when you want to have a little hygge time, the phone goes off, social media and news take a hike, and you give your attention to the here and now.

- FEELING GOOD: Enjoy that tea or coffee, revel in those decadent little chocolates that you love, put on your favorite music, take up your knitting, draw in your sketchbook, write a poem; do whatever activities you know make you feel great. Hygge is about indulging in those things and savoring the experience of simple pleasures in the moment.

- SHARING: Hygge can be experienced on your own, but it's also a great thing to share with others. That coffee is great, but it's nice to have someone else enjoy it, too. Does your family love those cookies as much as you do? Break them out and indulge together!

- HUMILITY: Hygge is not about competition or spending lots of money. Its pleasures are simple, familiar, and, often, the more homespun, the better. Do you have a treasured blanket or stuffed animal from childhood that you won't part with? That's hygge, so revel in those simple things.

- **THANKFULNESS:** Being grateful for what we have, rather than what we think we want is a natural part of hygge. And being grateful for the security around us and the space we've created for these moments is one of the best feelings we can have.

- **COZINESS:** Think warmth, color, comfort, taste, and smell—all the things that make you feel good and secure. Often these feelings are most obvious during the winter months, when we can hear a storm outside and know that we have our own little corner of the world that nothing can touch. Coziness brings out gratitude and feelings of safety, too.

- **FRIENDSHIP AND CLOSENESS:** Hygge is at its best with others. Now, there's nothing wrong with having some hygge time on your own, especially after a long day. But the chance to share the experience with family or friends can also be enriching and lovely. Hygge can be especially good for introverts, who might not be thrilled about going to a noisy party but would welcome inviting over one or two friends for an evening of wine, popcorn, cake, and movies. Hygge with others can be whatever you want it to be, and that's the beauty of it.

HYGGE IN YOUR HOME

For Danes, home is really where the hygge is. They even have a special word for it (of course they do): *hjemmehygge*, or "homeliness." Given that so much of hygge is about feelings of safety and security, it stands to reason that your home is the first and best place for you to enjoy hygge to the fullest. Your home is where you'll have most of your hygge experiences, because you can tailor it exactly to what you want it to be. We all hope that our homes are safe havens against the world, and on a cold day, we may want nothing more than to come home and curl up on the couch, eat some good food, and binge a few episodes of our favorite TV show. Believe it or not, that's already a kind of hygge! You're seeking out a safe place to let your proverbial hair down and just be, and that's part of the essence of hygge.

But what else can you do to make your home more inviting and a place where you can have that experience regularly or even daily? Wouldn't it be great to know that when you come home from work, you have your own little retreat that you've customized just the way you want it? Of course, you've probably already done a lot to personalize your abode; the suggestions in this chapter will help you add that little bit extra to make your home even cozier!

But you may be worried that you have to do a lot of work or fork over a bunch of money to get things in shape. It's not necessary to spend a lot of money to deck out your home. This goes against the spirit of hygge, anyway. You don't need the latest and most expensive décor; you need what's going to make you feel safe and happy. Using what you already have, plus a few small additions, can turn your home into a cozy haven that you'll never want to leave (one of the only downsides of hygge!). Here are some suggestions.

- CANDLES: Candles are basically essential for hygge. They are wildly popular in Denmark throughout the year, but especially in the cold winter months when days are short. They provide a warm, atmospheric glow that somehow lights up a room perfectly. There's no need to go out and splurge on expensive candles or scented ones (Danes tend not to like scented candles too much, anyway). Even tea lights and inexpensive candles can do the trick. Of course, you need to be careful, and never leave them unattended, but having a few well-placed candles in your main room will make a big difference to its ambience.

- **OTHER LIGHTING:** Hot, blaring, bright lights are against the concept of hygge, but there are plenty of options even if candles aren't really your thing, or you aren't able to burn them for safety reasons. Think about how you can use dimmer lighting to help set a better mood. Maybe try turning off the main lights and using a small lamp placed in a corner? Or using LED tea lights, warm twinkly lights, or white Christmas lights. These are cheap and can provide great ambience.

- **BOOKS OR OTHER MEDIA:** Do you love to read? You probably already have (too) many books! And you may have them arranged in shelves in various places. Feel free to accent these and showcase them: place some in "standing" position next to others that are stacked up, arrange by color, put a few in a nook or unusual space, stack near a nonworking fireplace, etc. Be creative! Maybe you have an impressive CD collection that you won't get rid of (awesome if you do!). Or maybe you have a collection of unusual objects you're proud of. Be sure to show these off in a way that makes them look good.

- **CUSHIONS AND BLANKETS:** Your couch probably already has a few cushions, and maybe you have a special blanket that you like to curl up under when the temperatures drop. If you normally only keep it on your bed, try bringing it out to the couch once in a while. Always have these at hand! Again, they don't need to be fancy or expensive; they just need to be things that make you feel comfortable. As Meik Wiking says, "What is better than leaning your head against a nice cushion while reading your favorite book?"

- NATURAL OBJECTS: Try getting a small bowl and put in a few items from the natural world. These could be pine cones, colorful fallen leaves, some dried flowers, pebbles, or scented potpourri. A little centerpiece for your coffee table, or even a shelf, adds a hygge touch.

- ANYTHING VINTAGE: Wood, copper, ceramic, it's all great! Do you have any antiques at home? Things you inherited? Something you picked up in a thrift store because you liked the look of it? All of these kinds of things are reminders of the past and can add a touch of nostalgia to your home. Use what you already have on hand, especially if you have any kind of emotional attachment to it.

- A FIREPLACE: You may or may not be lucky enough to have a fireplace in your home. If you do, and it's in working condition, it's well worth making use of it! Almost nothing says hygge like a crackling fire on a cold winter night. The sound of popping and hissing wood—whether in the stillness of the night, or against the wind and the elements—while knowing that you are safe inside is one of the best hygge experiences you can have! If you don't have a fireplace, worry not. You can still create that warm coziness with these other suggestions, and it will make candles even more necessary and appealing. Many online streaming services and websites now offer "virtual fireplaces" that "burn" for hours. One of these can be a great option if you long to see flames crackling but can't have them in your home.

- A HYGGEKROG: OK, this one isn't technically a must, but it's very nice if you can make it happen. A hyggekrog is a nook or a special place in your home that you can retreat to. It doesn't have to be a specially designed alcove or closet, or other location. It can be whatever makes you feel happy and snug. It can be your favorite blanket and a cushion or two on the couch. It could be an old comfy chair that you adorn with said blanket and other things. Maybe it's a breakfast table by a window that overlooks a garden or a nearby forest. It's simply a place that makes you feel happy and able to experience hygge in the way that's best for you.

HYGGE IN THE WORLD

It's all well and good to talk about having hygge in your own personal space, but what if that's not really an option for you? There might be any number of reasons that you can't decorate your living room the way you want it: you might be in short-term accommodations, or living in a dorm room, or any other reason. Is it possible to capture some of that lovely hygge feeling in other places? Happily, the answer is yes! And if you can indulge in hygge experiences at home, it's perfectly fine to bring that feeling with you when you're out. Here are some suggestions for how to bring the coziness and comfort of hygge with you almost anywhere you go.

- **EXPERIENCE HYGGE AT ANOTHER HOME:** If you can't set up your own living space the way you'd like right now, remember that hygge is not only about the setting. If you go over to visit a friend in their home for an evening of hanging out, good conversation, snacks, and laughs, you can experience hygge just as well as you would at your own place. We're not talking about formal dinner plans here; hygge is all about causal and comfortable. Having a few good friends can be essential to your experience, so reach out to them, if you're lucky to have them in your life.

- **FIND HYGGE OUTDOORS:** While hygge is all about safety and comfort, there are times when being outside brings out those same feelings. Maybe sitting on a beach, alone or with friends, and watching the waves roll in is something that brings you immense joy. Bring a drink and a snack, and you have a lovely afternoon ahead of you that captures much of the hygge spirit. Do you like camping? Sitting around a fire with a friend or two, sharing food and laughs, is a hygge experience. Even going for a walk in the park can do the trick. But it doesn't even need to be that elaborate. Going for a walk at dusk and watching the fog and mist roll in over the rooftops can be hygge, if you love it. Getting up to see the sunrise can be hygge. The natural world is very well suited to cozy experiences!

- **ENJOY HYGGE AT YOUR FAVORITE PLACE:** Is there a café you love that makes the best lattes? Or a little restaurant that serves your favorite food? A bookstore where you can sit in a comfy chair and just browse and read for as long as you want? These are all great examples of hygge away from home. Seeking out these little refuges when you can will give you further chances to experience hygge away from your personal space.

- **HAVE SOME HYGGE AT THE OFFICE:** Seriously? Sure, why not? While hygge at home is a retreat from the cares of the world, you can still bring some of that magic into your work. Making your workspace friendlier and cozier for yourself is only going to help you when the days get long and drag, or you're under stress to get something done. Can you dress up your cubicle a bit, with reminders of coziness and comfort? A plant or some photos, or LED tea lights? Can you organize a weekly tea and coffee break, where people bring sweets and share stories? Be creative and consider approaching your boss about ideas to "comfort up" the space a bit. Let them know it could very well improve morale and productivity, and they might just go for it!

- **PRESERVE HYGGE WHEN TRAVELING:** Travel can be super fun, but it can also be stressful, and sometimes you might just need a little reminder of home when you're far from it. This doesn't mean that you can go lighting tea lights on an airplane or starting a fire in your hotel room. Companies tend to frown on things like that. But when you are out, for business or pleasure, it's nice to bring something along that gives you that feeling of security and comfort. Some people bring along a favorite pillow or blanket so that the hotel room doesn't seem as sterile and unfamiliar (we all know how difficult it can be to sleep in a new hotel room on the first night!). Or maybe you have a little book of poetry that inspires you. Think about bringing along something that will give you that sense of comfort.

HYGGE AT THE HOLIDAYS

As you've probably figured out by now, hygge is tailor-made for the December and January holidays. In Denmark, there's even a word for it: *julehygge*. But "holidays" can mean anything that is special to you. It might well be the whole Christmas season, which in the Northern Hemisphere takes place in the colder, darker months, but if you live in the Southern Hemisphere, your best hygge experiences might come in July and August. Maybe you're not interested in celebrating the December holidays at all. If you're a Hindu, Diwali and the time around it might be the perfect chance for some hygge, since it is quite literally the "Festival of Lights" and celebrates the triumph of light over dark. The same goes for Islam and Eid al-Fitr; in fact, breaking the Ramadan fast with family and friends could be a very hygge experience. Many modern pagans have eight celebrations throughout the year. But whatever you believe or don't believe, there are times when you may be more in the mood for some hygge than others, and that's fine. These suggestions are mainly for the December through February months, but there's no reason you can't modify and adapt them to your own needs and wishes.

- ACCEPT THE STRESS: This may sound contrary to the whole point of this chapter, but there's a lesson to be learned. For many (most?) people, the holidays can be a very stressful time. The rush to make preparations, shop for gifts and food, worry about running up expenses, and so on, are all very real concerns. It seems like every year, we tell ourselves we're going to do it differently, but we keep falling back into the same stressed-out patterns. And you know what? That's OK. Hygge by definition stands in opposition to the stresses of the world, so in order to get to that space of coziness and safety, we may need to feel some discomfort. The way many Danes see it, hygge must be put off until the preparations are done, which is what makes it more special when the time comes.

- CUT DOWN ON EXTRAVAGANT GIFTS: One Danish trait when it comes to gift-giving as it relates to hygge is to keep it as equal as possible. Typical gifts might include food (especially baked goods and candy), drink, candles, flowers, simple household decorations, handmade items, and so on. Danish holidays are much more about good food and company than gifts. Someone who gives too many expensive gifts can be seen as boastful and superior, and may make the receivers feel that they owe something to the giver. If someone doesn't have much money, they may feel left out because they couldn't contribute in the same way. Presents are not competition, and no one should use them to try to make someone feel guilty or bad. The best things in life aren't things, after all.

- AIM FOR QUALITY OVER QUANTITY: Just as with gift-giving, it's not about how elaborate your holiday meal is or how many people come to your party. A simple meal that everyone contributes to, and which is enjoyed with genuine friends or close family members, has just as much feeling and will be appreciated as much as some big bash. It should always be about the time well spent, the good conversations, and the feelings of goodwill.

- **CREATE AND CELEBRATE TRADITIONS:** You probably already have some beloved family traditions that are trotted out every year at the holidays. Some of these may be great, and some may be terrible; there's always that one person that brings an awful food item that everyone has to pretend to like! The holidays are a perfect time to try introducing some new activities, especially those that are more aligned with hygge. Light up some candles. Make a new holiday drink that everyone will enjoy. Commit to trying some new foods. Play a silly game. All of these things can become new traditions, if people take to them and they enhance the seasonal mood. Get creative and brainstorm with the others to see what might go over well.

HYGGE IN EVERYDAY LIFE

Hygge is so obviously centered in the northern winter holidays that you might be wondering what you can do when those happy days have passed and the reality of the long winter slog of January sets in. It's no secret that people can feel down and depressed after a busy and exhausting holiday season, but self-care during this time is, if anything, even more important. January and February can have very short days in some northern regions, weather that makes you never want to get out of bed, and all sorts of lovely things like cold and flu bugs flying around. If you're having a case of the after-holiday blahs, there are many things you can do to keep the feeling of hygge going in the months ahead. Try out some of these suggestions and see if they can help you keep the spirit of hygge alive all year round!

- COMFORTING LIGHTS: In the darker months, candles and mood lighting are even more essential. Nice lights don't have to end with the holidays! Keep a stash of inexpensive candles on hand to light your way when you're in the middle of February and spring seems like a distant hope. Conversely, some gentle summer candlelight can only enhance the mood.

- TV NIGHTS: This is one of the most obvious choices, something you can do on your own or with friends. We've all become much more acquainted with binge-watching shows during the Covid-19 lockdown. And having time with yourself or with family to enjoy a cherished film or a favorite TV series can be just the thing at any time of year. Whether alone or together, make popcorn, break out your beverage of choice, and dive into your best movie or TV experience!

- **POTLUCK DINNERS:** One of the great things about having friends over for dinner is the chance for everyone to contribute. This takes all the pressure off one person playing host and providing all the food (unless you really enjoy doing that sometimes, then by all means do!). Come up with themes: pick a cuisine, pick one kind of food made in different ways, do an all-snack meal, etc. Get creative and see what comes up. In the summer months, this might be a barbecue or a picnic.

- **INEXPENSIVE WINE TASTINGS:** If wine is your thing, it's possible to host tastings that won't break the bank. Have a few friends over and have each bring one bottle of something to share. Again, this can be organized in many ways: by varietal, by country of production, by year, under $15, etc. This is a great way to try out new wines you may never have had or even heard of before. If wine's not your thing, beer is good, and so is cider. You can use nonalcoholic drinks, too. A tasting of cordials, zero-ABV cocktails, fresh-pressed juices, or even teas can be a fun way to spend an evening.

- BOOK CLUBS: Do you love mysteries? Or maybe epic fantasy and science fiction? Why not have a few friends all agree to read the same book and get together for a chapter-by-chapter discussion, with drinks and snacks? Everyone could commit to, say, reading two chapters a week, which should be manageable for most. As you work through the story, you may discover things about the plot and characters that you hadn't thought of before and gain new insights into the work. Book clubs work for fiction and nonfiction—pretty much any book you'd enjoy talking about with others. Book clubs can also be done remotely, so you can have friends in other parts of the country or world join in.

- WALKS AND BIKE RIDES: If weather permits (or even if it doesn't!), grab a friend or two and get outside. You can go for a walk in the country or explore a part of town you've never seen before. Is there a museum or art gallery with a new exhibition? Go see it! This can be fun for a small group or even for taking yourself on a "self-date." Likewise, if you have a bike, make the commitment to get out on it a little more, on your own or with others. It's great exercise and may just give you some hygge moments that you'll remember for a long time. The Danes are famous for their love of bicycling: in Copenhagen, over 60 percent of commuters go to work by bike. There are five times as many bikes as cars in Copenhagen, and it's believed that 90 percent of all Danes own bicycles. Use these exmaples as your inspiration to get out and get cycling!

- STARGAZING: Why not go out at night and look up? Gather a few friends or family members together and go someplace where you can get a great view of the night sky. Obviously, this works much better away from the bright lights of the city, but if you're fortunate to have access to a place that's a little darker and more rural, this can be a great way to have a lovely experience. Try it out at different times of year and see how the night sky changes over the months. As always, bring a snack or some drinks (nonalcoholic if you're driving!), and let the evening become a memorable one.

- GOSSIP NIGHTS: OK, this doesn't technically have to be about gossiping; it can just be a great chance to catch up. Sit down with some snacks and a few drinks, and see who's been up to what. Again, this kind of activity can be done in a small group in person or online via video; the online option is especially great if you're trying to reconnect with people who live far away from you. Again, you can have a theme, or it can be a general gabfest.

- GAME NIGHTS: We all love games. And having a regular night set aside for board games is something that almost everyone will look forward to each week or every few weeks. Or maybe you're into role-playing and want to get your D&D or Call of Cthulhu on! This is another activity that can be done in person or remotely, and can be an ongoing activity that brings a sense of hygge to your life.

These suggestions prove that hygge is very often about forming and keeping deep connections with others, which only enhances the whole experience. But it may be that you're introverted, not very social, or maybe just don't have a lot of friends or family at the moment. If so, you can probably come up with your own ways for how to do some of these activities. There's nothing wrong with making your favorite food and curling up with a good book on your own. That kind of self-care is just as important.

And when to comes to socializing, you might be even keener on having online get-togethers. The good news is that hygge often works best when it's one-on-one or a small gathering of three or four people, which is a "people number" that most introverts do very well with. Introverts tend to get exhausted at large parties, but an evening of food and drink with two friends with whom they are deeply connected can be one of the best things on offer.

You are no doubt well aware of your own likes and dislikes, so tailor your hygge experiences to the way you want them.

HYGGE FOODS AND DRINKS

The food and drink recipes listed in this book's other chapters are all perfectly good examples of things that you can indulge in when you want a little bit of hygge. Fika (the Swedish coffee break) and hygge overlap in many ways, of course. But you don't need to go out of your way to make elaborate foods to bring to your hygge experience, unless you really want to. When the whole point is comfort, comfort foods can be some of your best choices. You may already have a lot of these, and you can pick and choose whatever is best based on your mood. Do you have any childhood favorites that you still sometimes get cravings for? A simple peanut butter and jelly sandwich can absolutely be hygge if it brings you happiness and nostalgia. Hot chocolate? Most definitely! With a few marshmallows floating on top? Of course!

But in the middle of the summer, a hot, warming drink might be the last thing you'd want! Do you like iced coffee or iced tea? Those can be great alternatives, as can fizzy drinks and your favorite juice or smoothie in a special glass. Changing your foods throughout the seasons is a great way to stay more in tune with the passage of time. You might even want to try eating seasonally for your hygge moments: eat only those foods that are in season for that time of year. This will give you a greater appreciation for what brings comfort during all seasons, as well as harkening back to much older traditions when we couldn't just get foods on demand. Of course, some foods, like chocolate, are fine at any time of year!

In short, there is no rule about how simple or elaborate your hygge foods need to be. Simply go with what you enjoy and don't worry about whether or not you're doing it "right." Just remember that the point of hygge is to savor the moment, indulge a little, and create spaces and times that are just for you and those closest to you.

CHAPTER 5

Lykke

Happiness Is All around You

(PRONOUNCED “LOO-KAH”)

DENMARK

"Happiness is being surrounded by wonderful people and feeling safe and secure."

—METTE ODDERSKOV

The point of lagom, friluftsliv, fika, and hygge should be to improve your life, and thus increase your happiness. But what does that really mean? What is it to be "happy"? The funny thing about happiness is that almost everyone will give a different answer about what it means for them. This is normal and as it should be. So how can one concept, lykke, bring everyone happiness? The answer is that it can't, or at least, it's not a cure-all. Think of lykke as a method, an attitude that you can use in your own life and circumstances that can increase your sense of happiness and well-being.

The Danes are repeatedly listed as being among the happiest people on Earth. At first this may seem obvious: a clean and modern country with excellent free health care, an efficient public transportation, free education for everyone, and many other benefits is bound to be a place that's happy. But it's less about those assets and more about the attitudes behind them. It creates a chicken-and-egg situation: Do these things make people happy, or do happy people create institutions that serve the public good, thus spreading around the happiness? It's a bit of both.

Remember, Denmark is also a northern European country with long, dark, cold winters, a lot of rain, and many days when you wouldn't want to go outside at all. And yet the happiness factor is still there. We've seen the effect that hygge can have to counteract bad weather and bad days, but is it possible that something more is also present in many Danes' hearts and minds? Is lykke, their happiness factor, something that anyone can tap into? The good news seems to be yes!

Meik Wiking is CEO of the Happiness Research Institute in Copenhagen, and he has studied and written a lot about Danish (and other countries') happiness. He is convinced that we can all access this idea in our own lives, wherever we might live. Most aspects of happiness are not exclusive to any one group or nation. They are available to us at any time if we can be open to them and make some life changes here and there. This chapter will look at some of the ways you can cultivate a more "Danish" way of thinking about being happy, and, with a little effort, bring extra happiness into your own life and the lives of your loved ones.

There's not one big secret, or some magic pill to take to take you to Happy Land. But as with the other concepts in this book, doing a bit here and there will help you change how you look at some parts of your life, and may be the boost you need to begin feeling happier and more content.

THE IMPORTANCE OF TOGETHERNESS

A key component of happiness is being with others of like mind, who share our interests, and who just like being around us. They are there for bad times and good and give us a sense of belonging. Family is often the first place where this security can be found, but for those who have difficult (or no) relationships with their blood kin, a chosen family can be an equally important alternative.

It's important to remember the difference between "loneliness" and "being alone." Having time to ourselves is very important, and most introverts crave this time as essential to their mental and physical health. Being on your own and feeling happy are entirely compatible ideas. Loneliness, on the other hand, is the feeling of having no friends, no one to turn to (or not often enough), and not feeling that you have anyone for support and encouragement. Having a social circle, even if it's only a few people, is essential to our happiness.

The Danes have a word for it: *fællesskabsfølelse*, which means having a sense of community. In Denmark and Iceland, over 95 percent of people say that they believe they can rely on others in their times of need. That's a very powerful and reassuring feeling for a society to have!

There's no doubt that loneliness is bad for our health. It can lead to depression or make existing depression and anxiety much worse. It can affect cognition, raise cortisol (stress hormone) levels, increase the risk of heart disease, affect sleep, and raise cholesterol levels. Clearly, this is not something we should take lightly. There are problems with increasing feelings of loneliness in our society, which social media and Covid-19 isolation have only made worse. So, what can we do to help foster feelings of community and inclusion?

- IF YOU'RE LONELY, TRY TO GET MORE IN TUNE WITH YOUR FEELINGS. Ask yourself what is wrong, what is missing, and think about ways you could fix that. Don't compare yourself to others; their story is not yours. Ask yourself how often you feel lonely, and if anything is triggering it or if it's a more general sensation. If you can identify causes, you can start to work on solutions.

- **TRY REACHING OUT.** If it seems that everyone is ignoring you or doesn't want you around, that might not be the case. Even in a time when so many people have been forced to shelter in their homes and can't have physical contact, people still get caught up in their routines. We all do it. The internet was supposed to connect us, but often, it seems to do just the opposite. Still, you can use it to reach out. Try sending a few messages to people you haven't chatted with in a while and see if you get a response. Often, people will get back to you, and be happy to catch up a little. It might be that they're feeling lonely, too.

- **TRY TO SET UP SOME ONGOING TIMES TOGETHER.** Whether or not a meetup is in person or via online video, email chat, or whatever, see if you can arrange a time for you and a friend, or a few friends, to actually take time for each other. Catch up on how everyone's week has been going and share your stories, even if there's nothing too exciting to say. Since the onset of Covid-19 and the reliance on video chat in place of personal contact, studies have examined the idea of "Zoom fatigue." Research shows that video sessions can indeed leave you feeling more tired. This has to do with video needing more of our concentration, but also the stressors of things like being sad about not being able to see loved ones in person. When it comes to connecting with others, you might want to try a combination of calling, texting, and video chat to see what works best for you, and to give yourself more variety.

- VOLUNTEER SOME TIME, IF YOU CAN. One way to decrease your feelings of loneliness is to feel needed by others. If you can spare an hour or two a week to help a retirement home, an animal shelter, or anything you feel drawn to, it can be a great way to forge some new connections with other volunteers, as well as the people you're helping out. Helping others leads to more happiness all around and is a great way to feel valued and needed.

- CONSIDER A PET. Countless studies have shown the beneficial effects on mind and body that come with having an animal companion. Of course, this is not going to be an option for everyone. You may not be able to keep a pet for financial reasons, or maybe you live in a place that doesn't allow them. In that case, if you're still fond of being around animals, try volunteering at a shelter, helping out with dog walking, or whatever else would get you into contact with furry (or feathered or scaly) friends. Animals can't be a total replacement for humans, but their presence can be calming, soothing, and enriching in its own wonderful way.

- CUT DOWN ON SOCIAL MEDIA. Ironically, these platforms that were supposed to bring us together end up making us feel more isolated. We feel bad or even jealous when we look at all the cool stuff everyone else is doing, and we get the sense that we're not nearly as interesting, so of course that's why we have no friends! The truth is that everyone likes to post their best selves on social media. It's a persona that people take on, just like wearing a fancy outfit or special makeup. So, limiting social media time can actually help people feel less lonely. Concentrate on a few good friends and don't worry about what the other 725 are doing. You probably don't really know most of them very well, anyway.

- **CONSIDER SEEKING PROFESSIONAL HELP.** There is no shame at all in seeing a qualified therapist to talk about your problems and concerns. If loneliness just won't go away, it may be time to talk to someone about it who can give you unbiased opinions and suggestions that can bring real help.

HAPPINESS IS HEALTH IS HAPPINESS

That health and happiness are linked probably seems obvious. But it may surprise you just how much they are linked. Unhappiness is linked to higher rates of heart disease, inflammation, more susceptibility to colds and flu, and shorter life spans, among other problems. Being unhappy is unhealthy!

The good news is that this relationship is something of a two-way street. The more your health improves the happier you will be, but also the more you can increase your levels of happiness, the more likely you are to have better health. Since so many of our modern health problems are aggravated by stress and worry, it stands to reason that if we can work to eliminate or diminish those problems, we have a good chance of upping our happiness levels and feeling better in the process.

If you have health concerns, you should always consult your doctor or qualified health provider. But here are some steps you can take to improve your health right away. You already know the obvious ones like quitting smoking and cutting back on junk foods, but here are some other ideas.

- **SLEEP BETTER.** Easier said than done, but we all know that sleep is vital to health. Chronic issues with poor sleep can indicate an underlying condition, and it's worth getting that checked out. As we've already discussed, take the time to actually get sleep, and set the scene before going to bed. Try deep breathing, meditating, a hot bath before bed, and anything that will help you unwind. Power down the laptop and the phone an hour before turning out the lights and let your mind disconnect from the day.
- **CUT DOWN ON SUGAR.** Yeah sorry, whether we want to hear it or not, getting rid of this pernicious drug can only help us. That may seem at odds with some of the other advice in this book about indulging in sweets for fika, hygge, etc.

But remember that one of the key philosophies is lagom: everything in moderation. Have that ginger cookie with your coffee, but don't have eight! Enjoy chocolate cake on a cold night with some hot tea—and stop at one piece. We have a tendency to eat when we are upset, and sugar can be one of the most appealing tastes then. Eat because it's a treat, not because you're trying to use food to escape. Be moderate and make sugar an indulgence because you deserve it!

- **MOVE MORE.** Take those stairs, ride your bike, get a standing desk. You may not be able to go to the gym four times a week, but getting your body used to the idea of doing some kind of movement each day will be great for you. If you work in an office, go out for lunch (taking those stairs!), and get in the habit of getting up once an hour or so to move, even if it's just to take a turn around the office. Tie it in with some task to do or question to ask of someone. The Danes are avid bike riders for a reason!

- **TRY SOME MEDITATION.** Meditation goes hand-in-hand with happiness and can be a wonderful way to help achieve inner calm and contentment. Various techniques have been used around the world for centuries and work just as well today, or have been modified to meet modern needs. Investigate some simple mindfulness exercises and try them out for a few weeks. Use the exercises in this book and see if they bring you to a place of feeling calm. A calmer mind will translate into a more relaxed body, and getting rid of stress is one of the key ways of improving one's health.

- TRY A GENTLE MOVEMENT EXERCISE. Millions have found that yoga, Tai Chi, and Qi Gong (among others) have definitely improved their health. There are many versions of all of these practices, some more difficult than others, but all three have simple beginning exercises that can be learned easily and used to build into more elaborate routines, if you wish. You don't have to be super bendy to try yoga, or super coordinated to do Tai Chi. Qi Gong often involves just standing in place, but can also be done while sitting. If none of these appeal to you, check into other gentle warm-ups and exercises, like Pilates. Or, if you really want to go northern European, check out *Stádhagaldr*, or runic yoga; these are standing postures based on the ancient Germanic and Nordic runes. Another great option is Nordic walking, an exercise that derived from skiing and trekking, and uses poles. It engages more of the body and is considered an excellent workout for all ages. Using one of these modalities daily will almost certainly bring benefits. Exercise is a natural mood booster, but it doesn't have to be strenuous or vigorous, if that's not your thing.

FEELING FREE

Freedom can mean anything from the status of the nation you live in and the rights of its people, to how much time you have to yourself. And there is no doubt that with feeling free comes a good degree of happiness. The Human Freedom Index is an annual report that ranks nations by the state of their freedoms. As you might expect, nations like Denmark and Finland routinely score high, while China and Iran score low. The United States usually comes in between about fifteen and twenty down the list. Where someone is born and lives can have a profound effect on how free they feel.

But assuming that you are living in a relatively free country, what are some of the other ways you can have more freedom in your life? A lot of it involves reclaiming your own time. Here are some ideas.

- **LOOK AT YOUR WORK SITUATION.** This is a big deal for most people. If their work-life balance is out of balance, they can quickly find themselves devoting way more time to work than they would like. And this isn't just about the hours worked. It's about commute time, work taken home, Saturdays given up, etc. If you're feeling overwhelmed by your work, it might be time to reassess what's important, and what's making you unhappy. Money is important, and job security is important, but if you're only living to work, your happiness is going to plummet, and fairly quickly. While Sweden and other Nordic countries are experimenting with shorter work weeks, you may not have that option, but try to claim back some of the time you do have with the following suggestions.

- **LIMIT SOCIAL MEDIA.** This advice again! Studies have shown that while social media is meant to connect us, spending prolonged times on various sites actually makes us feel worse, not only about the time we're wasting, but also when we read about all of these wonderful lives everyone else seems to have. Just remember that many people are putting their best faces forward on these platforms, and their amazing updates are probably not indicative of what's going on in the rest of their lives. Use social media sparingly and with caution. No one is as happy as they appear to be.

- **MAKE BETTER USE OF THE TIME YOU DO HAVE.** Going hand-in-hand with getting off of social media, try to use the time you do have more effectively. Prepare your work lunches over the weekend, freeze them, and have them ready for the whole week. Then you have more time in the workweek evenings to do what you want to. Even getting thirty minutes back of "you time" will let you feel more in control, and freer.

- **GIVE YOURSELF DEADLINES.** So, you need to clean up your place over the weekend? Good, but get more efficient at it. Don't let it eat away your whole Sunday afternoon. Imagine that you have relatives coming over in an hour and you need to get it all done. It's amazing how much more efficient we can be under a deadline! If you only have an hour to do the vacuuming and dusting, you'll get it done. And the upside is that you then have more free time for the rest of the day!

- **UNDERSTAND THE CHALLENGES OF PARENTING.** The so-called Parental Happiness Gap is real. It's a measure of how parents compare their levels of happiness to their friends who don't have children. And yes, more often than not, parents report feeling less happy, due to the lack of time and freedom that being a parent can bring. But parents aren't doomed to unhappiness—not at all. Children in and of themselves are a great source of joy, and feelings of happiness often increase as the children grow up. In countries that have "communal parenting" (i.e., regular help with children from grandparents and others), levels of parental happiness tend to be much higher. If, as a parent, you have others in your life that might be willing to help you out, try seeking them out more often. Freeing up even a little bit of your time might be just the boost you need to feel freer and happier.

Freedom is something of a subjective concept. Some things in our lives that feel like constraints and traps may not be viewed that way by others. Using these suggestions as a guide, ask yourself what it is you need to feel freer.

FINANCIAL HAPPINESS: IS IT POSSIBLE?

We've all heard that money can't buy happiness, and we tell ourselves this, even if we don't necessarily believe it. The thing is, it's actually true. Vast amounts of money rarely buy happiness for anyone. There is a concept in economics called the law of diminishing marginal utility. What this fancy term means is that a thing is always most desirable when we don't have it, and when we do, it can be great for a while, but the more of it we get, the less satisfying it is. Say you win the lottery and go out and buy a fancy sports car. It's awesome, but you don't just want one, so you get another, and then another. By your third or fourth car, they're probably not so exciting anymore. This idea works even with simple things: the seventh cookie is not nearly as satisfying as the first one, and you'll probably end up feeling sick. But what happens is that people buy more and more, desperately trying to re-create that initial euphoric feeling. And most often, they can't.

What money *can* buy is a greater feeling of security, and with it freedom. And the desire for that should not be diminished or dismissed. But all too often, people find themselves caught up in the trap that making more money is the ultimate goal, with no thought of what that might mean, or even what the point of it is. Because, really, once you have all of your needs met and feel safe and secure, how much more money do you need? $1 million? $5 million? More? At some point, the diminishment sets in and making money can become an empty goal in and of itself, almost like a pathological hoarding disorder. But assuming that you're not a multimillionaire, here are some ways of thinking about money that can contribute to your overall happiness.

- BUY EXPERIENCES, RATHER THAN THINGS. Countless studies have shown that blowing money on a $3,000 watch produces very little long-term satisfaction, but spending the same amount on a great trip to Paris will give you a lifetime of memories from the experiences enjoyed there. Traveling to a new place or trying out a new sport appeals to our desire for novelty, whereas that Rolex will probably get old quickly. Great experiences give us better value for money overall, because they speak directly to our emotions and sense of well-being. Even just splurging on the occasional nice meal will be of great value, especially if it's something shared with others. The Danish holiday custom of simpler gifts but great food and dinners is a lovely example to keep in mind.

- **LET BIG EXPERIENCES HAVE TIME TO GROW.** Planning a trip to a place you've never been before? Start planning it a year in advance, so you have time for the anticipation and excitement to build. Having something to look forward to during that time will give you a sense of money well spent, and an extra dose of happiness.

- **IGNORE THE LATEST FADS.** Do you really need the latest phone or gadget? The most expensive sports shoe? Probably not. Advertising agencies spend billions convincing you that you do, and the Fear of Missing Out sets in. It's all manipulation and lies to separate you from your money. Hold on to your cash and use it for something more personal and meaningful.

- **ENJOY THE PROCESS.** The goal may be to get the promotion to make more money, but don't make that end goal your only focus. Take the time to appreciate what you're doing in the moment. If you're working hard, give yourself credit for that. If you're planning the dream vacation, enjoy taking the time to make sure that it's going to be the best trip it can be.

- **DON'T COMPARE YOURSELF TO OTHERS.** Wherever they may be financially is due to different circumstances than yours. Feeling resentful or needing to keep up with your friends or colleagues is a surefire way to plummet into unhappy land.

- **IF YOU HAVE WEALTH, DON'T FLAUNT IT.** Seriously, almost no one cares, and those that do are probably just resentful. There are other, better things to spend your money on. It's also considered pretty tacky in the Nordic countries, and with good reason.

- **ACCEPT THAT YOU CAN'T CONTROL EVERYTHING.** You may be careful and frugal with your money, but things still happen. Accept that risk is a part of life and that economies boom and contract, jobs come and go, and you may not always be in the same place you are right now. If you look at the process of having and using money as one of learning and growth, you can be prepared regardless of what happens.

In general, a majority of Danes have responded to surveys saying that they expect to be happier in five years' time than they are now. This isn't about making more money, per se, but rather a general cultural and societal expectation. Whether they're richer or poorer, they expect their happiness to improve as they grow and experience more of life. This is a great idea to live by!

KINDNESS AND TRUST

Having a community to rely on can be a considerable boost to overall happiness. Whether this is with your family, the neighborhood, or society at large, trust is a state that brings feelings of security and safety. Knowing that someone else has your back can give you great peace of mind. So how do you build feelings of trust with others? Be trustworthy yourself, and treat everyone kindly and fairly. Once again, making others happy brings happiness to oneself, and being reliable and trustworthy will almost certainly open the door for others to be the same for you.

In 2015, the World Happiness Report noted that "A successful society is one in which people have a high level of trust in each other—including family members, colleagues, friends, strangers, and institutions such as government. Social trust spurs a sense of life satisfaction."

The Danes often display remarkable trustworthiness. It's not at all uncommon for parents to leave their infants outside of shops and restaurant in their strollers. Yes, they are left unattended. No, almost nothing bad ever happens. It is such a deeply ingrained part of the culture that no one thinks anything of it. That's a deep level of trust! And while we might not have nearly as much trust where we live, we can work to improve trust with our friends, neighbors, and larger communities by being true and being kind. Here are some suggestions.

- KEEP YOUR WORD. If you tell someone you're going to do something, do it. It's that simple. In the same way that you deliver a project on time at work, be as diligent about delivering a promise to your friends when they're relying on you. The more trustworthy you become, the more people will be willing to trust you. Conversely, don't make promises that you can't keep; be realistic, no matter how much you might want to be helpful.

- LISTEN AND GIVE YOUR FULL ATTENTION. When someone is talking to you, listen and take a genuine interest in what they're saying. This builds rapport and feelings of friendship, as well as greater trust over time.

- ADMIT WHEN YOU'RE WRONG. It's the adult thing to do, and it will be far better for you in the long run. It shows that you have humility and are trustworthy. Trying to deny or cover up mistakes will get you nowhere. Never blame others for your own mistakes.

- LEARN TO TRUST OTHERS MORE. This can be very hard if you've come from a background of being mistreated or betrayed, so be gentle with yourself on this one. Try letting someone do something for you once in a while, no matter how small. Over time, you might just get used to the idea that you can trust others, even a little.

- PRACTICE EMPATHY. Always be kind. Always try to see things from the other person's point of view. Resist the urge to be critical unless it's truly warranted. Read more fiction; interestingly, being able to empathize with characters in a story has been shown to improve our own ability to empathize in real life. Always remember that everyone has their own story, and it may be very different from yours.

- PRACTICE RANDOM ACTS OF KINDNESS. It can be fun to secretly do something that improves a person's day. There's no limit to what you can do in this regard: smile and say a friendly hello to everyone in your office (and mean it). Send an email to a friend telling them you were just thinking about them and how much you value them. Take a friend to lunch, your treat. Compliment someone on something you like about them. Introduce yourself to the new person in the office and make them feel welcome. Tip a little extra for the overworked barista. Buy a small gift for your friend and give it to them just because. Buy a sandwich for a person experiencing homelessness. Help without being asked to; just see a problem and get to work on it (assuming it's allowed by your work and the law, of course!).

- GET MORE INVOLVED WITH YOUR COMMUNITY AND WIDER WORLD. Are there simple things you can do for your neighborhood that would help others? This is a great way to build trust while acting kindly. In England, an anonymous individual named the Free Help Guy took this idea much further. He started up a practice where he simply asked people to email him when they needed help with something. The response was overwhelming, but he went to work and has done enormous good for many people, all for free. He's done everything from help people find renters to try to locate long-lost relatives to looking for donors for operations and transplants. He does it all because it makes him feel good, and it's probably safe to say that he's a lot happier than most people!

How we interact with others has a lot to do with how happy we are. The Nordic countries in general have done a good job of building up levels of societal trust and a sense of the common good, so that people can get on with living their lives and not feel unsafe. But no matter where we might live, we can import some of those same ideas and practices into our own lives and make ourselves happier.

CHAPTER 6

Sisu

Courage, Grit, Determination, and Acting Rationally in the Face of Adversity

(PRONOUNCED "SEE-SU")

FINLAND

“[Sisu] is within the reach of everyone. It lies within you.”

—JOANNA NYLUND

Sisu is an old idea that has become very popular in Finland over the last hundred years. As with so many of these terms, it's not quite translatable, but probably derives from the Finnish word *sisus*, which means "guts," and that gives you a good idea of the sentiment that goes along with it.

It's a concept that embraces ideas like resilience, courage, tenacity, and being able to face adversity. Finland is a beautiful country, but one with harsh winters, and one whose people have endured hardships, invasions, and control from foreign countries. The Finns fought for and regained their national identity beginning in the nineteenth century and into the twentieth, when they finally won independence from Imperial Russia. They know a thing or two about adversity and struggle, and yet Finland continually shows up at the top of lists of happiest countries in the world. Many people believe that sisu has a lot to do with that.

Sisu is something that Finns often say they feel rather than speak about. To say that someone "has sisu" is considered a great compliment. But one should never brag about "having" sisu; that goes totally against Finnish character. If you have to talk about how tough or brave you are, then you don't have sisu. Sisu is not shown by talking about it; it's shown by getting on with things. Your actions are what show sisu.

The good news is that the Finns don't have a monopoly on sisu. Anyone can exhibit its traits, and you certainly have many times in your life, if you think about it. Cast your mind back to remember any difficult situations that you faced. Were you able to rise to the challenge and overcome them? Then you've shown sisu. It's not some mystical, magical power that we can only hope to have access to. Sisu is already around us and in us; we just need to learn how to cultivate it better, so that we can be ready when difficult situations come up.

But be aware that sisu is not about achieving great things. If you finish a marathon, that's not sisu. Sisu is the determination to put one foot in front of the other to begin with. It's facing a difficult situation without being certain of the outcome, but finding the courage to face it anyway. And no matter how much we wish otherwise, moments like that will fall into our lives. We try to keep ourselves insulated and comfortable, but sometimes fate just intervenes. And we are forced to step up, whether we like it or not. Sisu is for those times.

The Finns like to point to the war with the Soviet Union in 1939–40 (known as the "Winter War") as a prime example of sisu as a part of the national character. The Soviets invaded Finland in November 1939, and the Finns were massively outnumbered. They had no hope of defeating a much larger force in open battle. They could have surrendered, but they didn't. They got organized and made a plan. They were skilled in skiing and knew the landscape much better than their invaders. They prepared their clothing with excellent camouflage, and launched a guerrilla counterattack that wore down the Soviets so much that they withdrew in March 1940, a little over three months after they invaded! The Soviet army had suffered a humiliating loss, and was forced out. Finland lost some territory but retained its sovereignty, and its reputation as a nation of badasses grew around the world! *The New York Times* even ran an article in 1940 that had the headline: "Sisu: A Word that Explains Finland."

When the invasion started, it all looked pretty bleak. No one could predict how things would turn out, but the Finns didn't give in to despair. They stepped up to the proverbial plate, made a plan, and put it into action, even though they knew there was a good chance they would fail. And the incredible thing is, they succeeded, probably beyond their wildest hopes! They saved their country and proved that a good dose of stoic determination can be the best bet against impossible odds. The story of the Winter War has been inspiring countless people ever since. It was a David and Goliath situation, with a similar outcome!

All of that sounds great, but you might be wondering how you can cultivate and incorporate more sisu into your own life. Happily, it doesn't have to involve putting on skis and going into the deep woods in winter to fight the enemy (and if you do need to do that for some reason, you might need a different book than this one!). But think about other challenges: Do you have a big test coming up? Are you interviewing for a job that you really want? Are you facing problems with a difficult coworker? Any of these everyday situations can call for a dose of sisu to give you the strength to confront and handle the problem.

Emilia Lahti of Aalto University writes that understanding sisu "reminds us that, as humans, not only are we all vulnerable in the face of adversity, but we share unexplored inner strength that can be accessed in adverse times."

Sisu in our daily lives is about cultivating determination (even a bit of stubbornness), the ability to think creatively, the willingness to fail and learn from it, and the commitment to face challenges head-on. It's also about being good to yourself, learning how to relieve stress, and training yourself to be prepared. Is it possible for sisu to be a bad thing? Yes, it can, if one becomes too stubborn and loses the ability to be realistic or compassionate with others and oneself. You can push yourself too far, and you have to learn how to know the difference.

All of this is easy to say, but how do you really draw on sisu for a happier, more fulfilling life? This chapter will show you!

TAKING ACTION WHEN YOU DON'T WANT TO

Having to step up and do something in an uncomfortable situation is probably one of the worst things we have to face in life, but the funny thing is, these times can seem terrible even when the situation isn't so bad! Again, we're usually not being called on to drive out an invading army, so why is it so difficult to put off doing things even though we know we need to do them? The answer is simple: fears and anxieties are totally normal and can leave us feeling overwhelmed before we even start.

The good news is that everyone goes through this struggle, so you're not alone! The Soviet army may not be a threat, but perhaps you'd rather let the earth open up and swallow you whole than get up in front of a group of people and make a speech you need to make at the end of the week. So, what do you do? What we all do: procrastinate, find ways of working on other things, make excuses about getting to it "later today," and any number of other things, just so we don't have to face up to it. But of course, this only makes it worse, and we end up worrying about it even more as the deadline looms, and we're even less prepared. This is a guaranteed way of making sure that our worst fears come true! Here's how you can draw on the concept of sisu to overcome this.

- GET READY: It pretty much goes without saying, but being prepared is the best way to face up to a difficult situation. Yes, that means being reminded of it constantly, but that's a much better option than putting it off until the last minute! If you need to make a speech, practice it over and over. If you have a job interview, practice what you'll say in the interview. If you're facing a difficult family situation, try to learn as much as you can about it. Talk with others if you need to: friends or family that might offer insights and advice. You're probably not alone, so lean on others for the support you need. The better you can go in prepared, the less awful the situation will feel.

- BE GOOD TO YOURSELF: This is often overlooked, but sisu isn't about powering through things no matter how bad they get. You're not a Norse god facing impossible odds—at least, you shouldn't be! You're not going to do yourself or anyone else any good if you're exhausted, stressed out, angry, and argumentative. The point is not to win at all costs, including costs to your health and well-being. The point is to be prepared for what comes at you and be able to face it with determination, preparation, and even some confidence. And you can't do that if you're tired and/or sick. So make sure that when a challenging situation comes up, you take the time to look after yourself as best as you can. There are some suggestions at the end of the chapter for how to do this, including simple meditations for achieving calm. Acquiring this kind of inner peace and strength will greatly increase your chances of staying in the moment and focusing on the task.

- **SEEK OUT STRENGTH IN NUMBERS:** The idea of sisu might conjure up the image of a lone wolf bravely facing adversity alone and triumphing against impossible odds. But most of us aren't superheroes. In order to really show our strengths, we have to admit our weaknesses, too, and that's really a show of sisu all on its own. And asking others for advice and help is a way of showing that strength. Seeking out others can spark new ideas about how to tackle problems and face adversity. Knowing that others have your back can be a great source of comfort. Keep in mind the Finnish proverb: *Ei kysyvä tieltä eksy*, which means, "Who asks for the road doesn't get lost." Ask for help.

- **REMEMBER THAT SISU IS NOT CONSTANT:** Sisu is not a permanent state to be in; it's a strength you draw on when the need arises. Trying to be in that state all the time, to suppress emotions, or to act as if nothing matters will only make you feel sick, tired, depressed, and discouraged. Being able to express and talk about our hurts and traumas is crucial. It's important to let go of sisu when it's time and be vulnerable and willing to feel what you need to feel. Never think that you're failing if you need a break or can't express heroic and stoic attitudes all the time. That's not how it works!

DRAWING STRENGTH FROM SISU

So, you may be reading this and thinking that this sounds good, but how does one actually draw on those reserves of strength to face the tough times? It's not just a matter of deciding to get on with it when the need arises. You'll have to cultivate some practices to help you, like going to the gym to strengthen your sisu! But fear not, this doesn't take huge amounts of time or effort. A little bit every day can help you be in a better frame of mind if or when challenges happen. You can tailor your prep to your own individual needs and circumstances; there is no "one size fits all," since we each already have our own ways of coping and reacting. But these suggestions will give you some ideas.

- **LEARN FROM YOUR MISTAKES:** We all make mistakes, and there's no shame in that. The real test of character is what we do about them. Sure, some will be embarrassing, or we'll know that we can do better and get angry with ourselves. Some mistakes are more costly than others, whether at work or in life, but it's crucial that we learn from them so that we don't repeat them. And yes, this can be much easier said than done, especially in personal and family issues. But being able to take the blame for something is a sign of strength and maturity. There's no need to beat yourself up; try it with little things first and see how it goes.

- BE OK BEING A LITTLE UNCOMFORTABLE: Our natural inclination is to seek out the safe and the comfortable; it's the whole point of hygge, after all! But sadly, we can't live in that state forever, which is what makes those hygge moments so special. Accept that discomfort is a part of life and be willing to roll with it, if not be happy about it. Maybe you have to commute to work on a dark, rainy morning. Not fun, but it's also not the end of the world. Resolve a few times a week to face up to life's discomforts with a more positive—or at least stoic—attitude and see how you do after a few weeks.

- GET OUTSIDE MORE: As you'll see, the Finns consider nature to be a very important part of sisu, especially the uncomfortable parts of it! But this doesn't mean you need to go camping in a thunderstorm or try hiking up the nearest mountain. Just resolve to get out a bit more and take in whatever nature is around you. There are many reasons to do this, as this book shows, but one of them is to give you a stronger connection to your surroundings, and an appreciation for both the natural world and the struggles of those who came before us, in the days before central heating and the internet.

- CULTIVATE A GOOD WORK ETHIC: This isn't just about doing your job well, though you should, of course. But it can also be about developing healthy routines in your own life: making sure the trash gets emptied and things cleaned, for example. Taking pride in your personal space takes work, and developing this through doing the work to keep it up is a very good trait to have in troubled times. Simple and small acts every day will help develop a stronger sense of the value of your work, both at home and your job.

- CULTIVATE YOUR FRIENDSHIPS: No one is an island, and it's important to have people to lean on when things get tough. Our strength truly is in numbers. It doesn't mean that you have to socialize constantly or maintain a vast friendship network; in fact, it can be just the opposite. Use your hygge moments with friends to deepen and develop those friendships, and make the commitment to be there for each other when needed. Lending a helping hand will then just be a natural extension of the togetherness you already enjoy.

- **EXERCISE:** You knew this was going to be here, didn't you? But don't worry, no one is going to ask you to start running marathons . . . not yet, anyway! But being able to move a bit can do wonders for body and mind, and put you in a better state to deal with problems. Feeling angry or frustrated about a challenge you're facing? A good workout might be just the thing to get it out of your system, so you can come back to it later with a fresh perspective, less clouded by emotions. Finland has more than 30,000 sports facilities around the country, and 90 percent of Finns take part in physical activity at least twice a week. Whether walking, hiking, skiing, running, sledding, or archery, there's something for everyone!

- **SET REALISTIC GOALS:** When listing your goals, make realistic timelines for achieving them. What can be done this month? In six months? In a year or two? Break down your biggest goals into smaller chunks so that they don't seem overwhelming. This will give you a much better chance of getting started on them and seeing them through. Set little milestones along the way and reward yourself with a hygge evening when you achieve one of them as an incentive to keep going!

- **BE WILLING TO TRY AGAIN:** The importance of perseverance and a willingness to fail are critical to developing sisu. You're going to fail sometimes; it's inevitable. That doesn't matter nearly as much as what you resolve to do about it. It's perfectly fine after a failure to sulk, to feel useless, or even to threaten to give up. Allow yourself to go through that yucky time, but tell yourself that when you've done so, you'll be ready to give it another go. This goes for personal and professional concerns. Of course, sometimes it's necessary to throw in the towel, but you'll get a better sense of that as you work through this.

DEVELOPING LASTING COURAGE

We probably all wish that we could handle things under pressure better than we do. But the truth is that we procrastinate, we ignore things that concern us, and we generally think that we're too chicken to ever step up and face problems head-on. More often than we'd like, we feel like the Cowardly Lion looking for our courage. The good news is that there are plenty of things we can do to help improve how we handle difficult situations that don't require making heroic efforts, walking on hot coals, bungee jumping, or having tarantulas walk across our hands. Here are a few ways you can cultivate your courage in easier ways, all of which will improve your ability to access your sisu.

- UNDERSTAND WHAT FEAR REALLY IS: Chris Bertish, a world-record-holding surfer, knows a thing or two about fear: "Fear is saying: this is the perfect time to be able to do what you're trying to do. Your body is actually preparing you to have a positive outcome. Once you can really understand that fear is an emotion like any other emotion, you can learn to manage it."

- ACCEPT THAT FEAR IS INEVITABLE AND THAT'S OK: You've no doubt heard it before: bravery is not the absence of fear. It's feeling the fear and doing it anyway. And while the idea may seem like a cliché now, there is much truth in this. Fear is a natural reaction; it keeps us safe from dangers, and our deep ancestors had a healthy amount of it for good reason. So, when you're facing an uncomfortable situation that you'll have to deal with somehow, tell yourself right away that your discomfort is a part of the process. It might never go away throughout the ordeal, but it doesn't have to rule you. Strive to make some peace with your fear and understand that everyone goes through the same feelings.

- **BE OK GETTING OUT OF YOUR COMFORT ZONE:** When it's time, set the hygge aside and be open to the idea that it's good for you to experience things that make you a little uncomfortable. This is one of the best ways to grow as a person, to learn new things, and to experience life as it might be seen by others. Resolve to do it on a regular basis by doing the following:

- **TRY ONE NEW BRAVE THING A WEEK:** Once a week, try to do something unusual that you've not done before or that makes you a little uneasy. Again, this doesn't involve trying a danger sport or signing up to help wrangle rattlesnakes. It might be as simple as taking a different route to work or the grocery store. Maybe you don't like talking to people all that much. Try just smiling and saying hello to one random person a week. That's not so terrifying, is it? Pick one week and try a new food that you've never had, and never really wanted to try before. The next week, start a conversation with a new coworker. There are endless ways to do this without it being a Herculean chore, and over time, your bravery will increase. You might even find yourself looking forward to the next week's challenge!

- **BE WILLING TO ASK FOR WHAT YOU WANT:** So often, we hide our own needs and downplay them as not being important. This happens in workplaces, in relationships, in friendships, and just about anywhere. Being able to express our needs to others can be uncomfortable, especially if we don't even feel worthy of them! Anything from asking for a raise to asking someone out on a date can bring out our anxieties, and pretty soon we're talking ourselves out of even trying. We all struggle with this, but try putting a few of these needs on your "brave new thing" list, and resolving to do them. Start small and simple. If you find this is a real issue for you, there is no shame in seeking counseling and therapy to get at the deeper issues. Anxiety is a real thing and needs to be addressed. That can be your brave thing to do!

- **THINK THINGS OVER BEFORE ACTING:** So often, we react to bad situations with an emotional response first. Again, this is probably hardwired into us as a survival mechanism, which may be good for avoiding lions, but isn't as great in the modern world. Get in the habit of stepping back and thinking things over for a bit first. Tell yourself you're going to take an hour or a day or however long to think on it before deciding or taking action. Sleeping on a problem might well give you a new perspective, and removing yourself from the heat of the moment will almost certainly give you a better result. The Finnish have a saying: *Aamu on iltaa viisaampi*, which means, "The morning is wiser than the evening." Give yourself the chance for a new perspective.

- **DON'T OVERDO THINGS AT THE START:** Don't expect that you're going to shed years of conditioning and ingrained behavior just because you want to. It's good that you want to get started, of course, but be patient with the process. You will fail, you will want to give up, and you will lapse back into fear. All of that's OK. Even after you feel like you've developed a hardier response to difficulties, there will still be times that seem overwhelming. Courage is not a destination, and each new challenge may test you in different ways.

- **BE ABLE TO MOVE ON:** Being able to let go of bad situations and people can be one of the hardest things we have to do, and will take all of our sisu to do. As you develop more sisu over time, you'll probably gain a better sense of yourself and a better feeling of self-respect. Knowing when to walk away from a challenge that can't be met is one more sign of sisu.

If you work on the items in this list, you may find that you'll be able to identity problematic situations before they even start, or recognize the kinds of people that shouldn't be in your life. We all learn from experience, and you'll probably develop a better "problem thermometer" along the way. After you've faced down one situation, you'll have more confidence that you can do it again.

THE IMPORTANCE OF THE NATURAL WORLD

Just like the Norwegians and their friluftsliv, the Finns have a great love of nature. In the Finnish case, it really takes over during the very long days of summer, when daylight can last anywhere from nineteen hours to the sun never setting, depending on how far north you go! There is an almost national obsession with getting back to nature during the summer months, usually involving going out to a rustic cabin, called a *mökki*, in the woods or by one of Finland's countless lakes. Many Finns own their cabins in the country.

The thing is, these cabins often don't have what we would consider modern conveniences: central heating, electricity, and even running water are nowhere to be found. But why? Because taking time to go out to one's cabin is an exercise in truly getting back to nature. The whole point is to have an exercise in sisu by avoiding mod-cons and experiencing nature more as it is, just as their hardy ancestors did.

Does this mean you need to plunge into your local wilderness for weeks on end and experience the world in a way totally against everything you're used to in order to cultivate your own sense of sisu? Of course not! What works for one culture may not work so well for another. But the idea of experiencing nature in the raw can be a great way to reconnect and help you build some inner strengths.

As the chapter on friluftsliv notes, there are many health benefits to plugging back in to the natural world. Those suggestions work equally well here, but if you want to make use of nature to cultivate sisu, you might want to take a more active role in your experience, beyond just "being." Try going for a walk in a natural setting. Before heading out, read up a bit on the local flora and fauna, and learn about the natural systems and features of the area. You might want to go out at different times of year, when the weather isn't so great. Get a feel for how nature is both beautiful and dangerous. It will help you understand better what our ancestors lived with, and the problems they had to overcome.

If you live in a city, getting back to nature may be more of a challenge. Understand that you don't have to get out into nature to develop a sense of sisu, but any effort you can make will only help you. As with friluftsliv, locate green places in your local area, such as a park, no matter what the size. You can still learn about your local area: Who built the nearby park? What trees were planted there? Does anyone know why? Become more knowledgeable about your immediate surroundings.

The Finns have a law called *jokamiehenoikeus*, or "everyman's right." It's a right-to-roam law that allows them to go anywhere in nature, provided they cause no harm and do not disturb others. This is a treasured right that Finns see as an important part of their identity and well-being, as well as for developing a sense of sisu. A whole country can't be wrong. Get yourself as in touch with the natural world as you can, and draw strength from that connection.

EXERCISES TO CALM AND CENTER YOURSELF

In order to face life's challenges, it's important to feel grounded inside. The Finns have a long tradition of perseverance and not giving up, which is understandable in their often harsh environment. But drawing on that inner strength can seem challenging all by itself. For Finns, one of the simplest ways to tap into inner strength and happiness is to go out into the wilderness and just "be" for a while. The natural world is important, but so is something we could all use more of: silence.

APPRECIATING THE VALUE OF SILENCE

Finns are famous for their love of the outdoors, and one of the best aspects of getting out into the vast Finnish wilderness is to experience it without the sounds and intrusions of the modern world. Wherever we may be, it seems we are constantly barraged with noise and can't escape from it. So any chance to get away from it and embrace the silence should be a wonderful thing. But for many, it really isn't. Introverts know the value of quiet, but many extroverts thrive on a world of sound and action. We're hardwired in different ways, so we have to go with what we're most comfortable with, but if you are an extrovert who recoils at the idea of simply sitting still in silence for a while, the good news is, it won't kill you. Yes, you're going to be asked to do it in this section, and you may find that it does have great value. Pluck up that resolve to try one uncomfortable thing this week and make enjoying the silence something to be challenged by, and maybe even enjoy!

Many Finns believe that sitting with each other in silence isn't awkward; it's just that people only speak when they truly have something important to say. But when they do talk, they expect your attention; it's very rude to interrupt anyone in Finland when they're speaking! Learning to cut down on the chatter in our mouths and minds can bring a new sense of inner peace and an appreciation of the moment. As we saw in the chapter on friluftsliv, if you go into nature with someone else, leave behind the talk about the world out there. Be in the moment and take in your surroundings. Cultivating this on a regular basis is really a kind of meditation that doesn't involve sitting in contemplation.

EXERCISES FOR CALM

If you can't just go out to a quiet natural place, here are some simple meditation-like exercises for calm when the world seems to be whirling around you. Doing one or more of these regularly, especially in times of stress, will give you a place of strength to come from, and allow you to face challenges with less emotion and fear.

- **BECOME AWARE OF YOUR PHYSICAL STATE:** How do you feel when you are stressed? When facing a challenge, do your fists clench? Do you sweat more? Do you feel tense? Do you get a headache? Simply being more mindful of these reactions will help you to better understand how you process an uncomfortable situation.

- **BREATHE:** When you are facing something that's upsetting or uncomfortable, practice one of the breathing meditations, such as square breathing. Just a few minutes of this will bring a sense of calm and can often shift your emotional response. The appeal of that fresh, clean Finnish air is a major attraction to getting outside.

- **IDENTIFY WHAT YOU'RE FEELING:** Give words to your emotions, because this takes them away from pure feeling and into thinking, which can help to get a better handle on them. If it's helpful and practical, write down what you're going through.

- **RECOGNIZE THOUGHTS AS THOUGHTS:** You may find yourself spinning out worst-case scenarios and racing to bad conclusions, which can keep you from taking action. Tell yourself that these are only thoughts. Take a deep breath and say something like, "These are just thoughts." Let them come and go as they will but understand that they're not real. You might want to keep in mind the Finnish proverb, *Joka vanhoja muistelee, sitä tikulla silmään*, which means, "A poke in the eye for the one who dwells on the past." What's done is done, and it's OK to let it go. With that in mind:

- <u>BE KIND TO YOURSELF</u>: Don't beat yourself up for reacting badly or having negative feelings. You wouldn't berate a friend for worrying about something, so don't do it to yourself. Fear and worry are normal reactions; it's how we deal with them that's important. Breathe deeply and say something like, "I am kind to myself in this moment."

- <u>SMILE</u>: Strangely, the simple act of smiling can enhance and improve one's mood, even if you're not in the mood for it! This is not laughing in the face of danger as a bear comes charging at you, but rather allowing your body to take over and help put things back in perspective. There's no need to walk around grinning all the time (the Finns would think this was weird, anyway!), but smile to yourself throughout the day and see if it gives you a mood boost.

- <u>USE AN AFFIRMATION</u>: Find a short phrase that resonates with you. It can be anything, but should be positive and should be about affirming yourself. Use it whenever you are facing difficulties, combined with some of the other exercises here.

- **BE GRATEFUL:** This one might seem more difficult or even frivolous, but it can help to take a minute to remind yourself of what you do have. It's easy in times of stress to pile on one problem after another as if we're proving to ourselves how bad things are. They may be, but it's also important to be mindful of what you're thankful for, too, because those things may help give you strength to face the problem, or even encourage ways of solving it. Finns frequently talk about how they are grateful for the safety and security they feel in their society. We can tap into some of those same feelings by remembering the things in life that we're grateful for.

The Finns have a saying: *älä jää tuleen makaamaan*, which means, "don't stay lying in the fire." In other words, you need to act to progress. You must get out of the "fire" of your problem so that it won't consume you. Finns believe strongly in taking action to improve things. You will always risk facing setbacks and being disappointed, but giving up is not the answer. Being in a calmer state of mind, appreciating what you already have, and tuning into the silence of your inner strength can all give you tools to move forward and face life's challenges.

CHAPTER 7

Þetta Reddast

Everything Will Work Out

(PRONOUNCED "THAT-TA RE-DUST")*

ICELAND

* *"þ" is the letter "thorn" for the "th" sound. It was common in English until the late Middle Ages, and is still used in modern Icelandic.*

"*Þedda redast* represents a certain optimism that Icelanders have and this carefree attitude that borders on recklessness. Sometimes it works out, sometimes it doesn't, but we don't let that stop us from trying."

—AUÐUR ÖSP

We'll end this little book by looking at a saying that's popular in Iceland, a hardy island in the North Atlantic, a land of long, dark winters, shifting geological plates, exploding rock formations, and limited resources. Yet it's one that also scores high on standards of living and overall happiness. In this harsh environment of volcanoes and northern lights, many Icelanders have developed a more carefree outlook on life, but it's not one that says, "Whatever, it's fine." Rather it's a belief that with effort unfavorable situations can be brought to a favorable outcome. Auður Ösp, founder of the travel company I Heart Rekjavik, says, "We just believe in our abilities to fix things. With the conditions we live under, we're often forced to make the impossible possible." Note that this doesn't always mean that everything works out for the best, or the way you want it to; it means that we can all make the best of bad situations.

The Icelanders' ancestors had a rich vision of the cosmos, dating from the time of the first people who sailed there from Norway in the ninth century. These stories and legends, written down in the Middle Ages, told of gods like Odin, Thor, and Freya, strong beings for a strong people. A key part of these beliefs was the end of all things, Ragnarök. This cataclysmic event would result in the destruction of the world, and the deaths of many of the gods themselves, as the forces of evil and chaos were unleashed. And yet, Ragnarök was not really a time to be feared; it was part of a natural cycle, just as autumn gives way to winter and becomes spring again. Viking warriors wanted to die in battle, for a chance to feast in Odin's hall in the afterlife and be a part of his army, which would fight the mighty evils at the end of all things. And after this dark time, new gods and new humans would be born, and an even greater age awaited the new world.

With this kind of belief deeply ingrained in the culture, one can probably see why a modern philosophy of everything being OK in the end would be popular. In fact, an increasing number of modern Icelanders find themselves drawn to these ancient beliefs, and the revived religion is growing at an impressive pace these days. The philosophy of the Vikings still has meaning today. Þetta reddast is not a naïve hope that nothing bad will happen, but a more mature acceptance that yes, things can and will go wrong, but we can get through them (maybe with a bit of sisu thrown in?). The people of Iceland have faced challenges from their earliest days in the ninth century (when groups of farmers fled Norway and persecution) through the nineteenth century: everything from war and colonial overlords to trade restrictions and even a ban on dancing. Oh, and freezing cold weather, then and now. Plus the whole island is packed with geological activity. Remember when the amazingly named volcano Eyjafjallajökull erupted a few years ago and brought air traffic to a standstill? Iceland actually has hundreds of small earthquakes every week. Lovely.

But still, everything works out. These days, Iceland is a super modern country with all the conveniences of the twenty-first century, and the lack of a lot of its problems. Does their carefree, can-do attitude contribute to this society? Very probably. Can you adopt some of this same attitude into your own life? Most certainly. Here are a few suggestions to finish off the book.

- ACCEPT THAT DIFFICULTIES ARE INEVITABLE. No matter how much we try, sometimes things will go wrong, what we hoped for won't work out, people and situations will disappoint us, etc. It's just part of being alive. Though we all know this intellectually, when problems do happen to us, it's still normal and natural to react in strong ways. And there's nothing wrong with feeling upset, hurt, disappointed, angry, or however we need to react. There will be good times and not-good times, and we'll feel differently about them.

- **DON'T FEEL BAD ABOUT FEELING BAD.** One of the worst things we can do is get angry with ourselves about how we react to difficult situations. Feel what you need to feel, but also be ready to put things into perspective.

- **YOU CAN'T NECESSARILY CHANGE SITUATIONS, BUT YOU CAN CHANGE YOUR REACTION TO THEM.** This is an old, almost clichéd point these days, but there's still truth in it. Some things are just beyond our control, but we can learn to control our responses. The meditations and practices in this book are a great place to start. By cultivating happiness, contentment, feelings of safety, and determination, we *can* become better equipped to be in the right state of mind for when problems drop in our laps. If you have a lovely little hygge nook to retreat to, or a sense of contentment with your place in the world, or the determination to take small steps to finish a task, the problems that do come up will very often not seem so overwhelming.

- **ASK WHAT YOU CAN DO RIGHT NOW.** You may not be able to fix everything right away, but what are some small steps you can take right now to get the ball rolling? There's almost certainly something you can do. Breaking up the problem into smaller chunks also makes it less overwhelming.

- **LOOK AT THE BIGGER PICTURE.** Some problems are truly big deals, and they shouldn't be minimized. But many of the things we get bent out of shape over are, realistically speaking, minor. For example, getting stuck in traffic is rarely a life-or-death situation, but it can be very annoying. If it happens once in a while, it's no big deal. But if you have to put up with it because you're commuting to work every day, it's a bigger issue. Can you live with that? If not, it's time to think about working somewhere else. For truly cataclysmic events, such as car accidents or damage to a home, those who go through these trying times almost always say that what matters most is the safety of their loved ones. Possessions can be regained, new cars purchased, houses rebuilt, but those you love are irreplaceable, and as long as you have them with you, nothing else matters nearly as much.

- **ASK HOW YOU'LL FEEL ABOUT THE PROBLEM IN THE FUTURE.** What will this problem be like in a week? A month? A year? Maybe you'll see that it wasn't so bad, or it's even something you can look back on and laugh about. If not, what will you at least be able to learn from it?

- **EMBRACE LIFE.** We are truly miraculous. Each of us is here against overwhelming odds, and we get to partake in this scary, messy, complex thing called life. And that's a privilege. Yes, things will go the wrong way. Yes, we will screw up. Yes, sometimes everything will suck. But how much better is it to have the experience than the alternative? Live, love, give, celebrate, and revel in what life has in store for you. In the words of that old wise one, Odin:

  "Blessed is the one who lives free and bold
  And never nurses a grief,
  For the fearful are dismayed by much,
  And the stingy one mourns about giving."
  — Hávamál 48

GLOSSARY

Here is a handy guide to some unfamiliar and foreign words and phrases.

AAMU ON ILTAA VIISAAMPI (FINLAND): "The morning is wiser than the evening." A proverb that advises sleeping on it before making a decision.

ÄLÄ JÄÄ TULEEN MAKAAMAAN (FINLAND): "Don't stay lying in the fire." A reminder not to stay in a bad situation.

ALLEMANSRÄTTEN (SWEDEN): A right-to-roam law that lets people go anywhere in nature, as long they cause no harm and do not disturb others. Very similar to laws in Norway (*allemannsretten*) and Finland (*jokamiehenoikeus*).

CHOKLADSNITTAR (SWEDEN): Swedish chocolate cookies that are traditionally cut into wedges perfect for dunking.

EI KYSYVÄ TIELTÄ EKSY (FINLAND): "Who asks for the road doesn't get lost." Never be afraid to reach out to others and ask for help.

EYJAFJALLAJÖKULL (ICELAND): A volcano in Iceland whose 2010 eruption caused havoc for air traffic in Europe.

FÆLLESSKABSFØLELSE (DENMARK): Having a sense of community, and people to trust and rely on.

FIKABRÖD (SWEDEN): Pastry for fika, such as cookies, cakes, cinnamon buns, and even sandwiches.

GLÖGG (SWEDEN): A centuries-old mulled wine popular during the holidays.

HÁVAMÁL (NORSE/ICELANDIC): Thirteenth-century sayings and proverbs about how to live a better life, attributed to the god Odin.

HJEMMEHYGGE (DENMARK): "Homeyness," a sense of feeling safe and cozy at home.

HYGGEKROG (DENMARK): A nook or special place in one's home to experience the comforts of hygge.

JOKA VANHOJA MUISTELEE, SITÄ TIKULLA SILMÄÄN (FINLAND): "A poke in the eye for the one who dwells on the past." What's done is done. Let the past go.

JOKAMIEHENOIKEUS (FINLAND): "Everyone's right." Jokamiehenoikeus is a right-to-roam law that lets Finns go anywhere in nature, as long they cause no harm and do not disturb others.

JULEHYGGE (DENMARK): The special kind of hygge that one can have at the holidays.

KAFFI (SWEDEN): Coffee.

KANELBULLAR (SWEDEN): Cinnamon buns.

KARDEMUMMABULLAR (SWEDISH): Cardamom buns.

KARDEMUMMAKAKA (SWEDISH): Cardamom cake.

KNÄCKEBRÖD (SWEDEN): Crispbread that is flat and dry, and usually made with rye flour.

LAGOM ÄR BÄST (SWEDEN): "The right amount is best." A proverb about moderation.

LAXSMÖRGÅS (SWEDEN): A smoked salmon sandwich.

MÖKKI (FINLAND): A rustic cabin.

NATURRENSING (NORWAY): Nature cleansing, also known as a nature bath; a way of feeling refreshed and renewed by being outdoors.

RAGNARÖK (OLD NORSE/ICELANDIC): The time of the end of the world and the of the great cosmic cycle.

SMÖRGÅS (SWEDEN): A small sandwich popular for fika, lunch, and snacks.

SMÖRGÅSTÅRTA (SWEDEN): A savory cake made out of sandwich fixings; literally, a sandwich cake. Popular for parties and get-togethers in Sweden, Finland, Iceland, and Estonia.

SMØRREBRØD (DANISH AND SCANDINAVIAN): An open-faced sandwich often made with buttered rye bread and assorted toppings, such as cold cuts, fish, and/or cheese and other spreads.

SPRITZ (SWEDEN): Butter cookies.

STÁDHAGALDR (GERMANY): A system of yoga-like poses using the Germanic and Norse runes, developed in the early twentieth century.

INDEX

ABOUT THE AUTHOR

Tim Rayborn has written over thirty books and dozens of magazine articles about various topics, especially on subjects such as music, the arts, history, business, and self-help; he will no doubt write more. He lived in England for many years and studied at the University of Leeds. He has spent time in Scandinavia and was thoroughly enchanted by the lands and the people, and their civilized way of life.

Tim is also a classical and world musician who plays dozens of unusual instruments from all over the world that most people of have never heard of and usually can't pronounce.

He has appeared on more than forty recordings, and his musical wanderings and tours have taken him across the United States, all over Europe, to Canada and Australia, and to such romantic locations as Marrakesh, Istanbul, Renaissance chateaux, medieval churches, and high school gymnasiums.

He currently lives in Northern California with many books, recordings, and instruments, and a sometimes-demanding cat. He tries to implement various Nordic ideas about happiness and fulfillment into his life, especially the whole hygge thing. Related to that, he's quite enthusiastic about cooking excellent food and enjoying good wines and spirits, though caffeinated coffee is, unfortunately, not often an option.

WWW.TIMRAYBORN.COM

PUBLISHING PRACTICAL & CREATIVE NONFICTION

Whalen Book Works is a small, independent book publishing company based in Kennebunkport, Maine, that combines top-notch design, unique formats, and fresh content to create truly innovative gift books.

Our unconventional approach to bookmaking is a close-knit, creative, and collaborative process among authors, artists, designers, editors, and booksellers. We publish a small, carefully curated list each season, and we take the time to make each book exactly what it needs to be.

We believe in giving back. That's why we plant one tree for every ten books we sell. Your purchase supports a tree in the Rocky Mountain National Park.

Get in touch!

Visit us at Whalenbooks.com or write to us at
68 North Street, Kennebunkport, ME 04046.